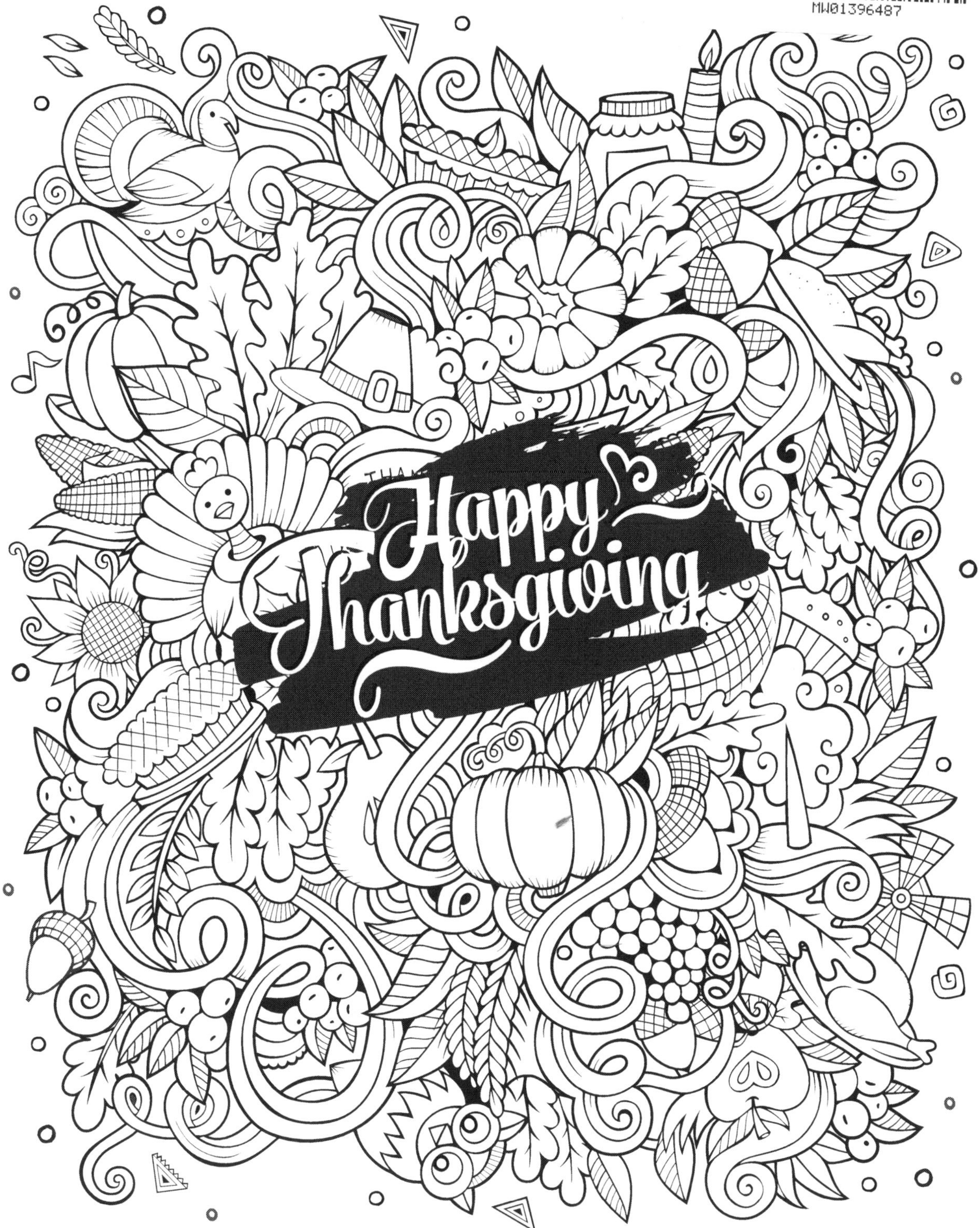

ADULT COLORING BOOK

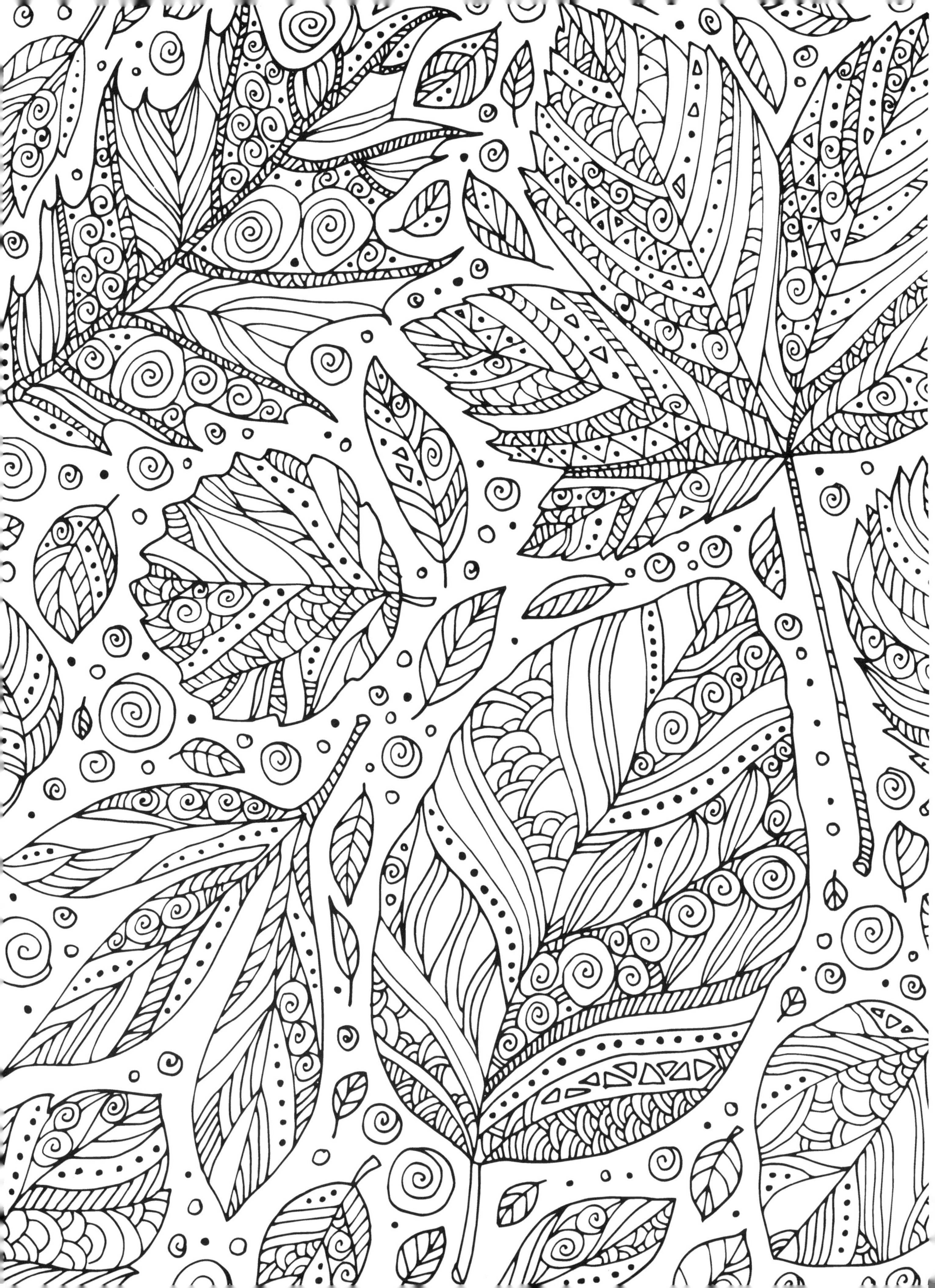

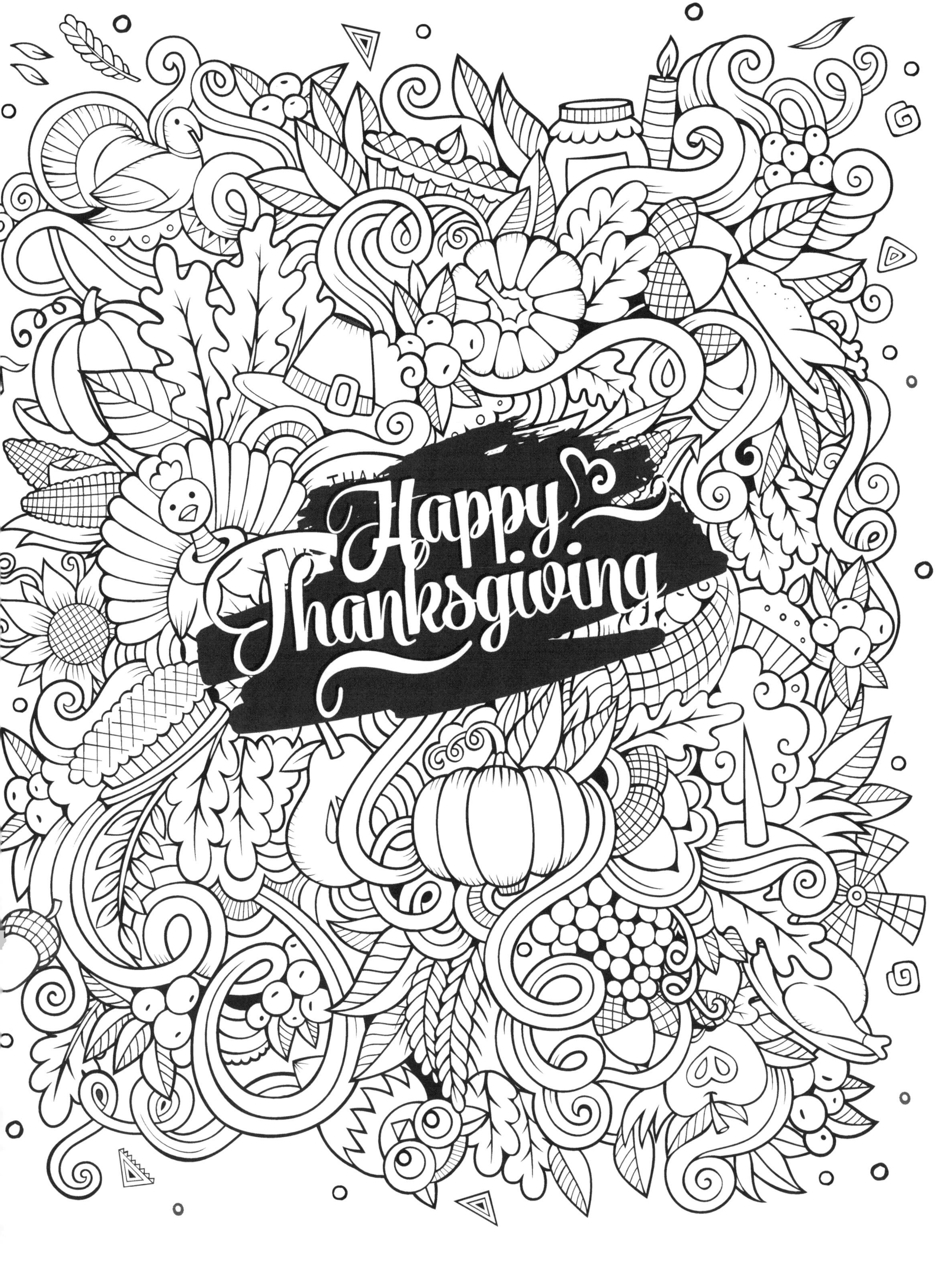
Happy
Thanksgiving

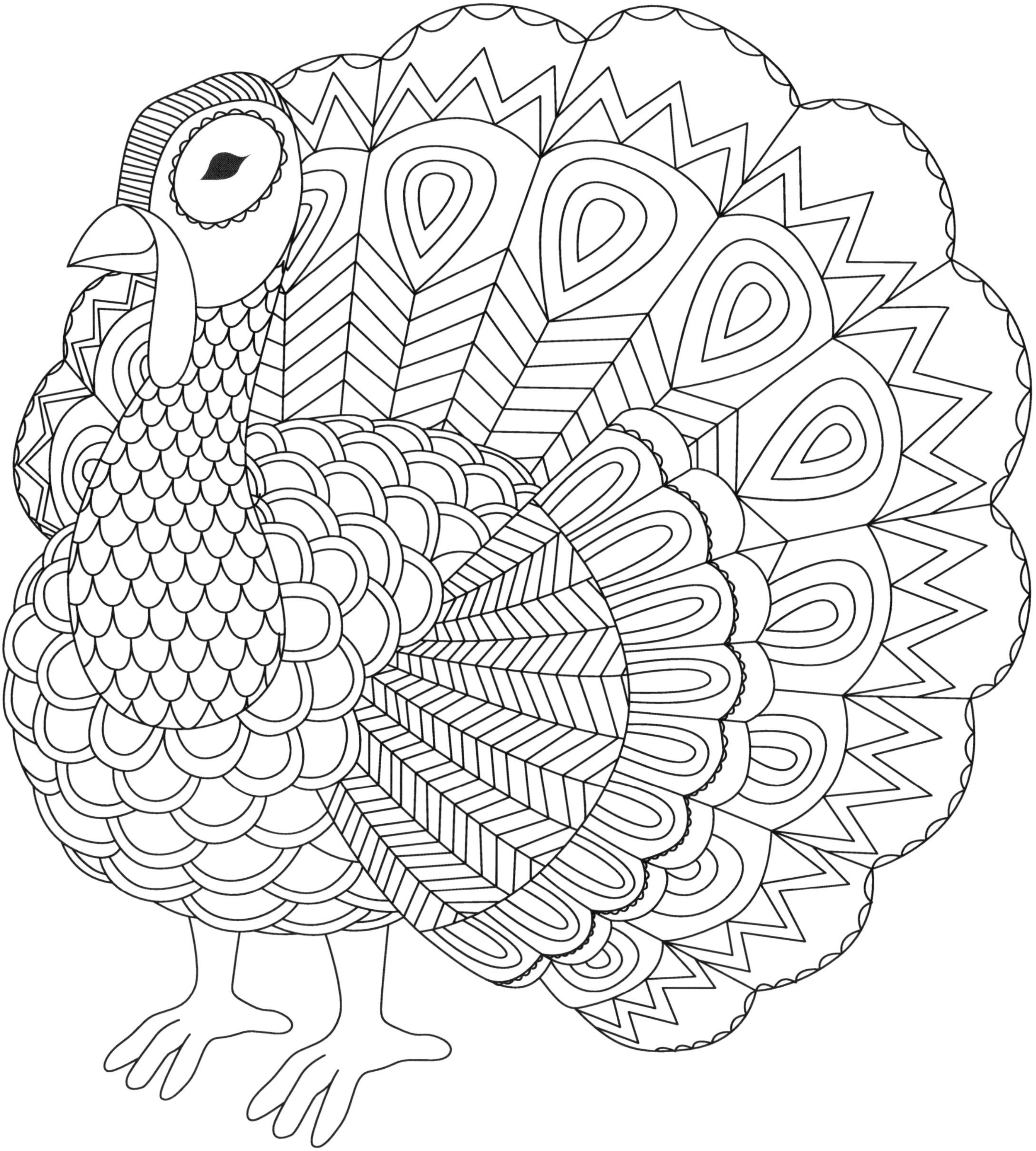

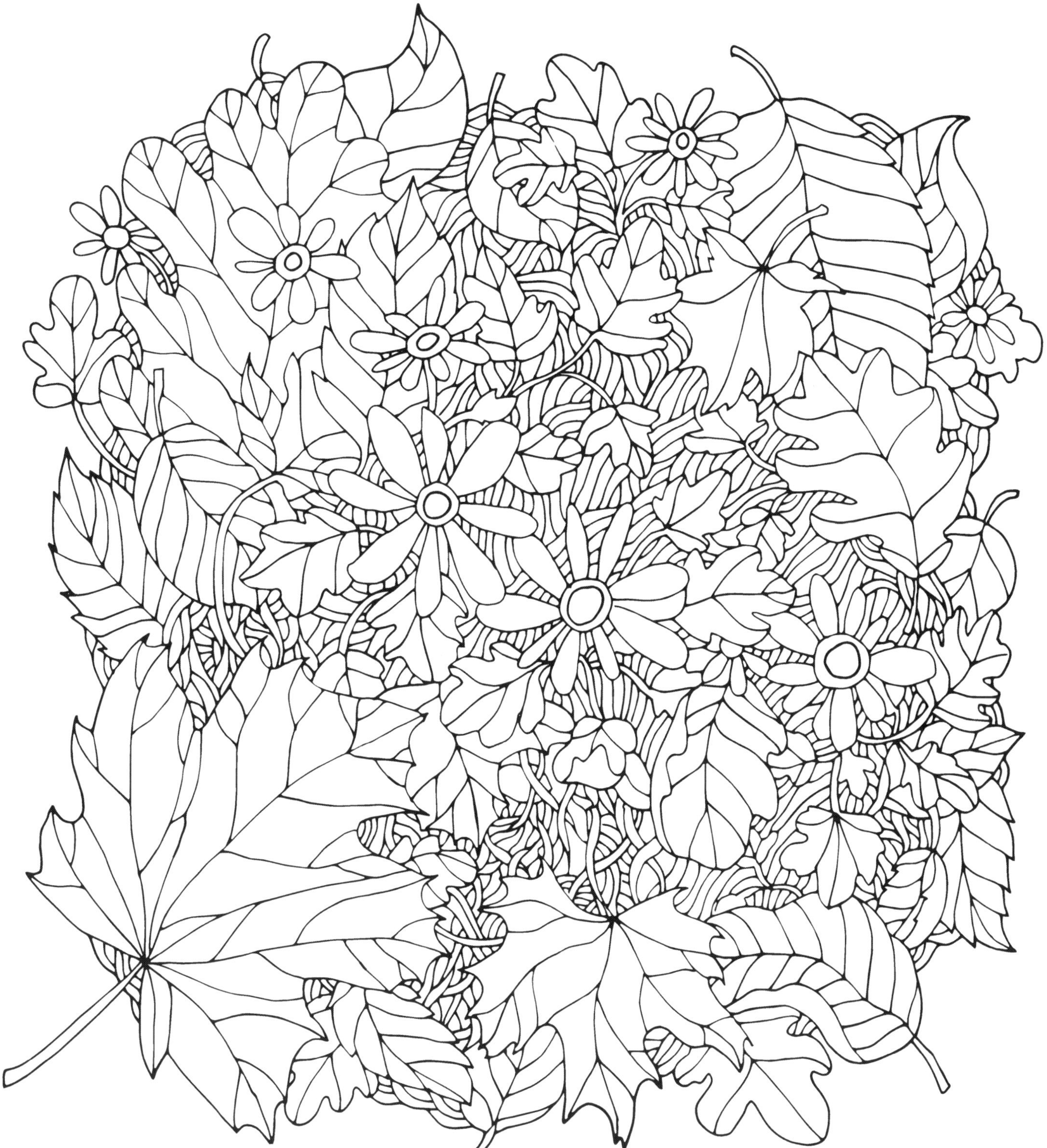

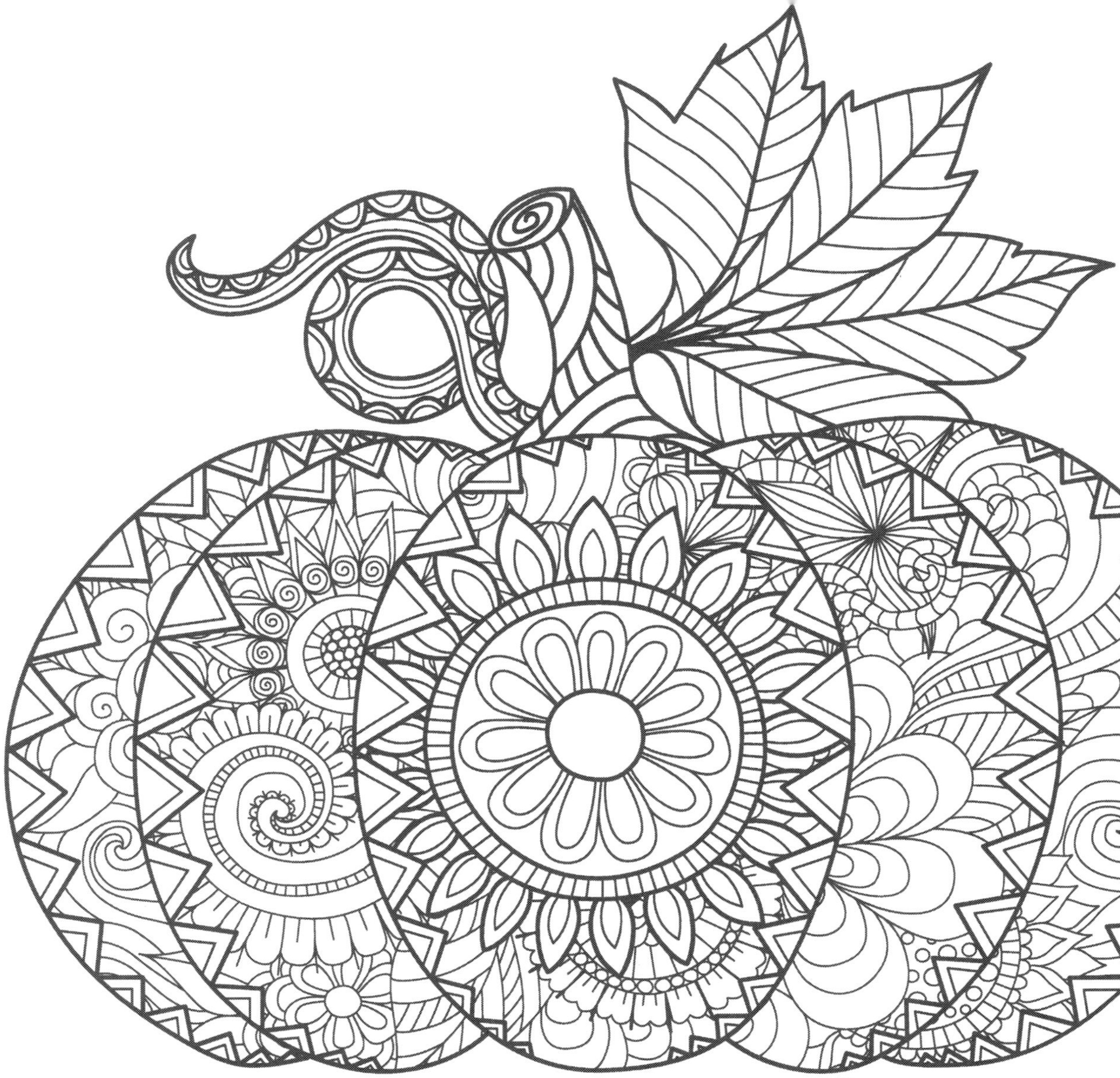

Happy Thanksgiving

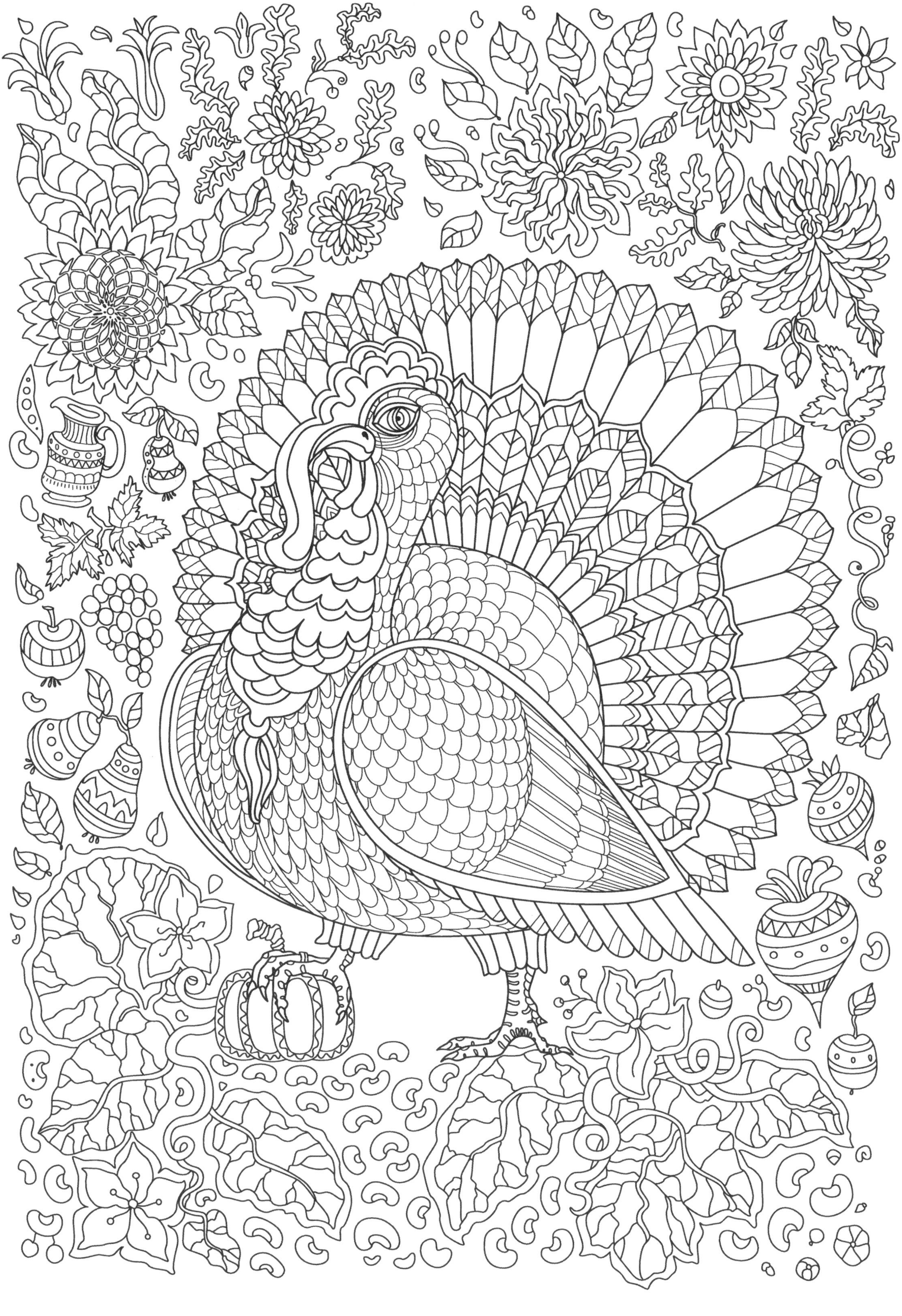

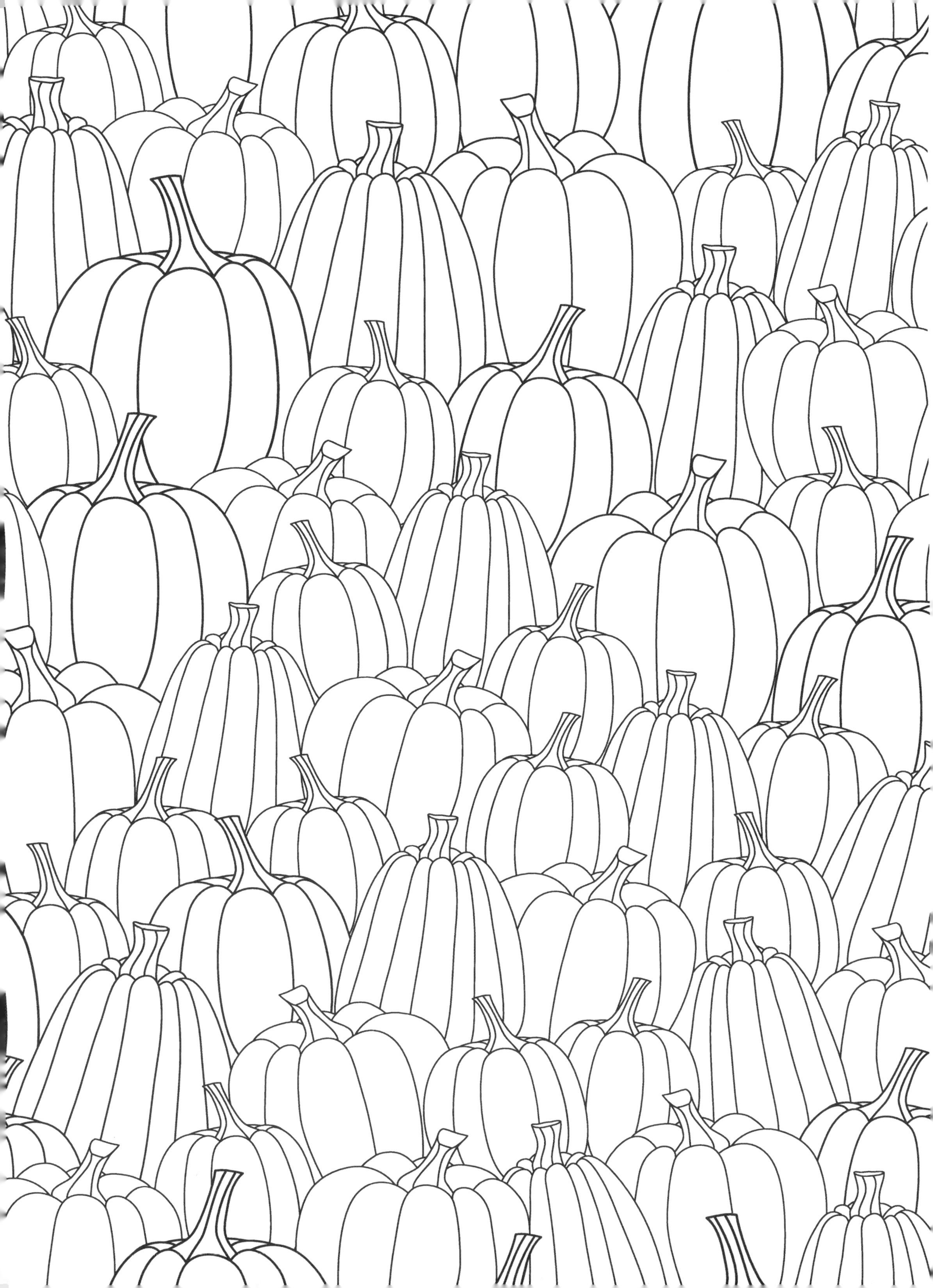

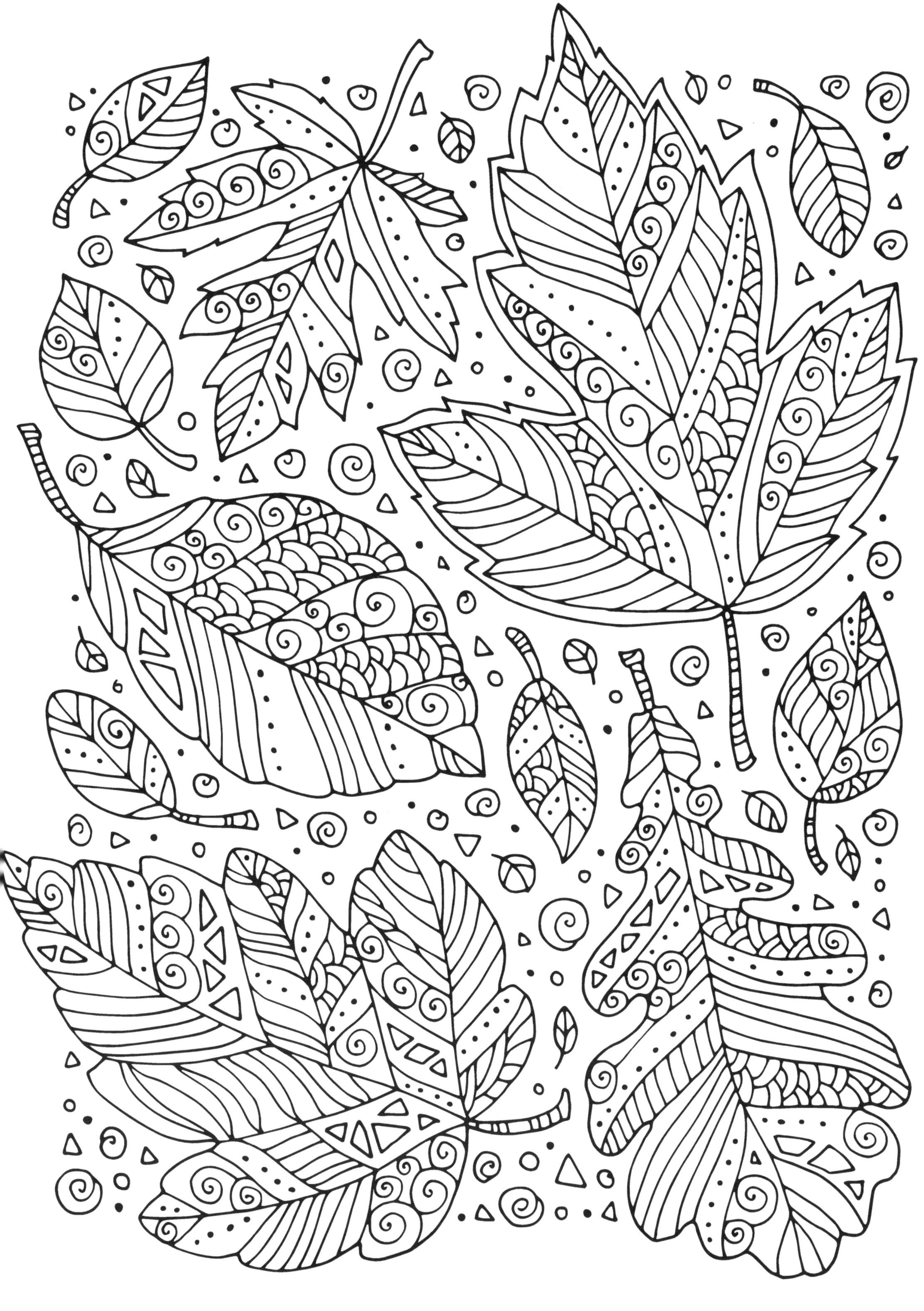

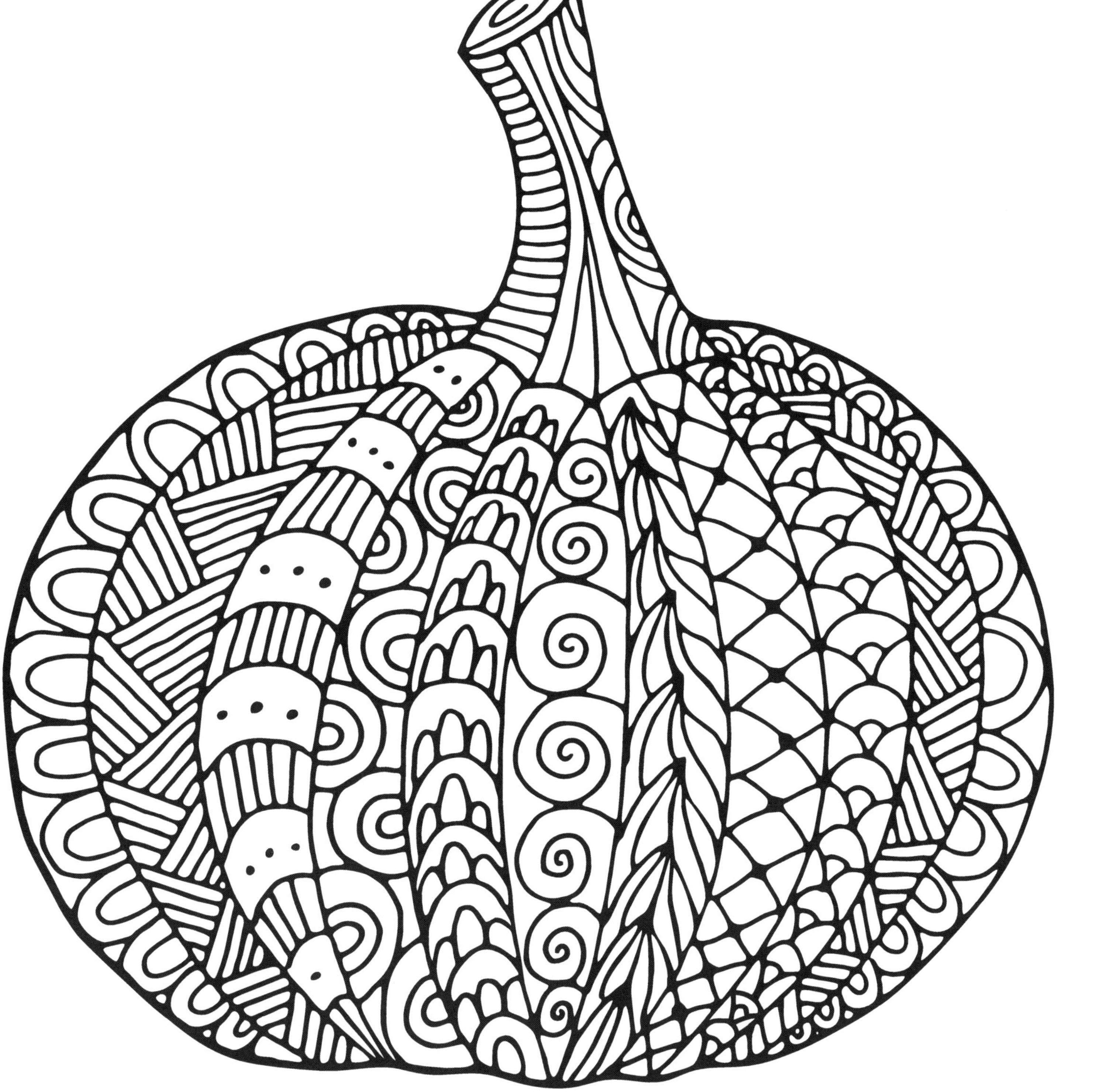

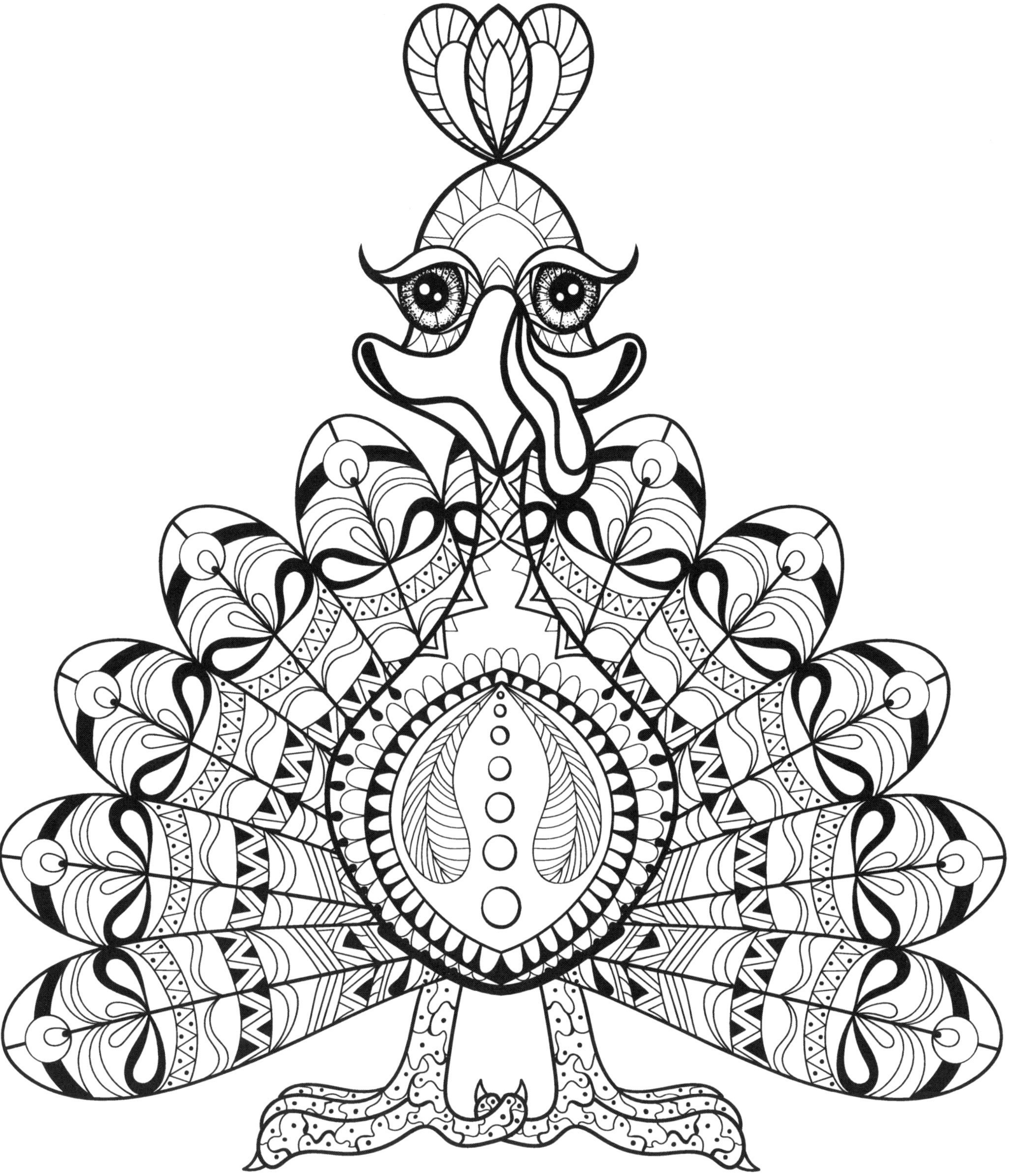

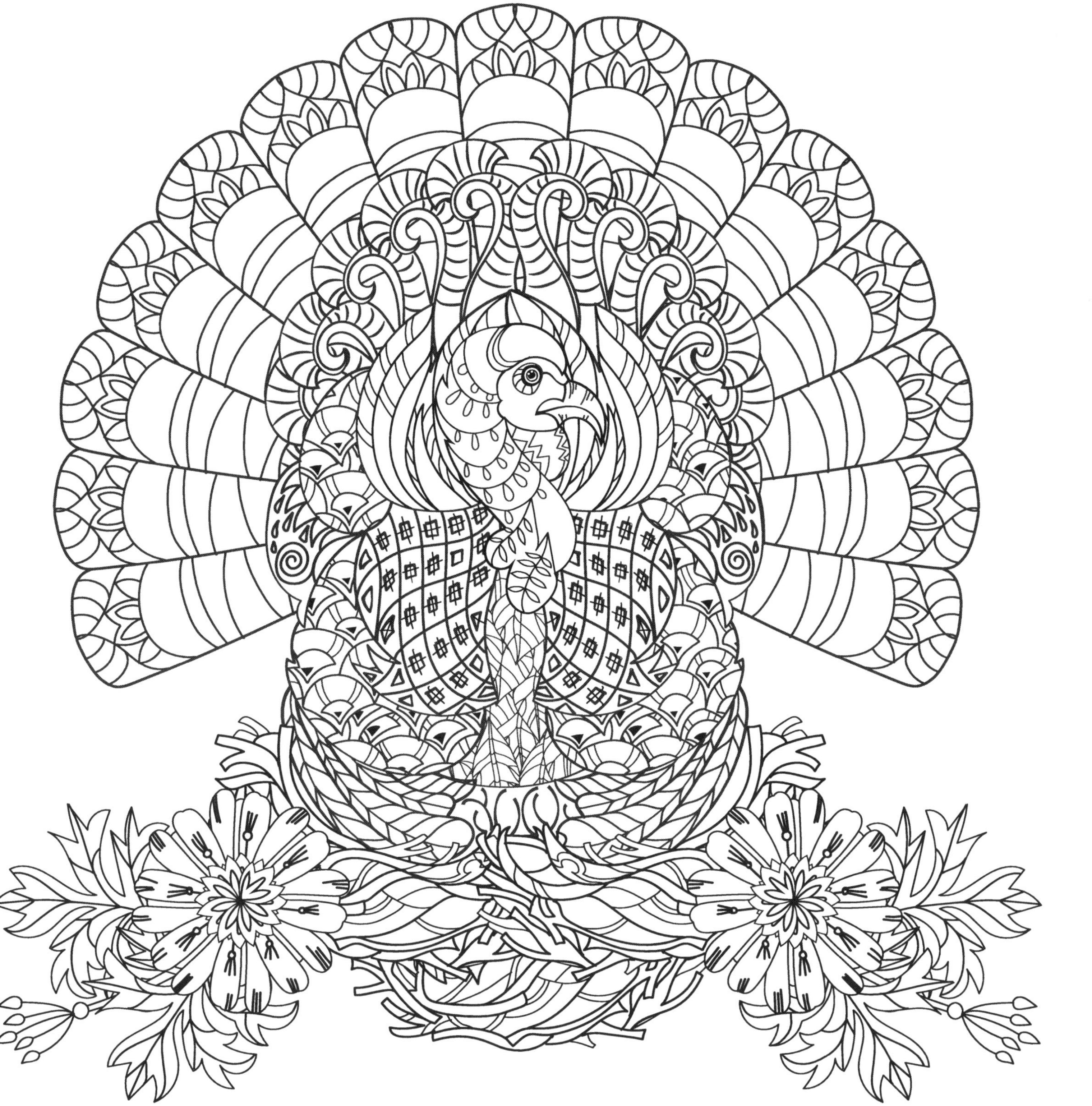

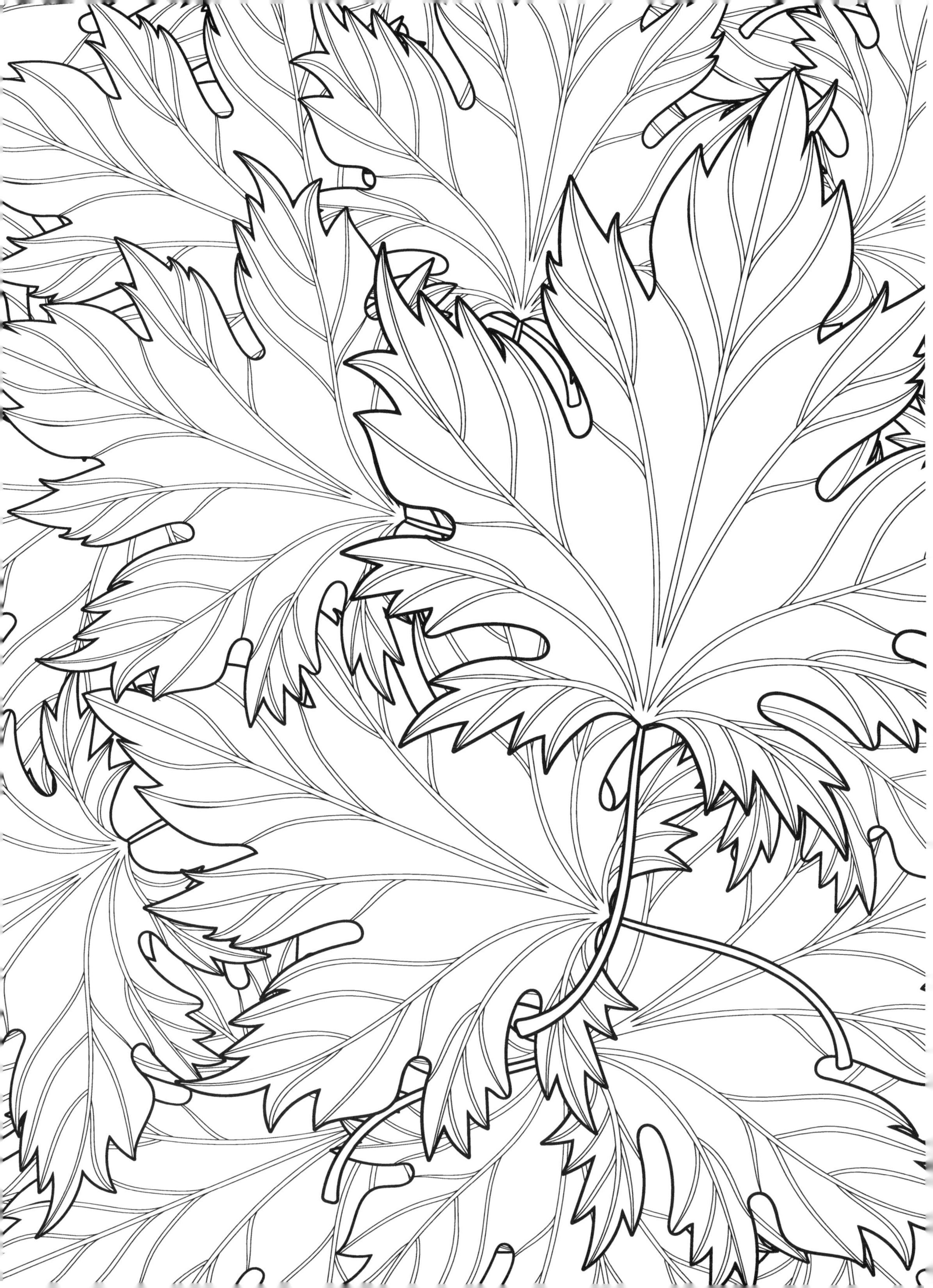

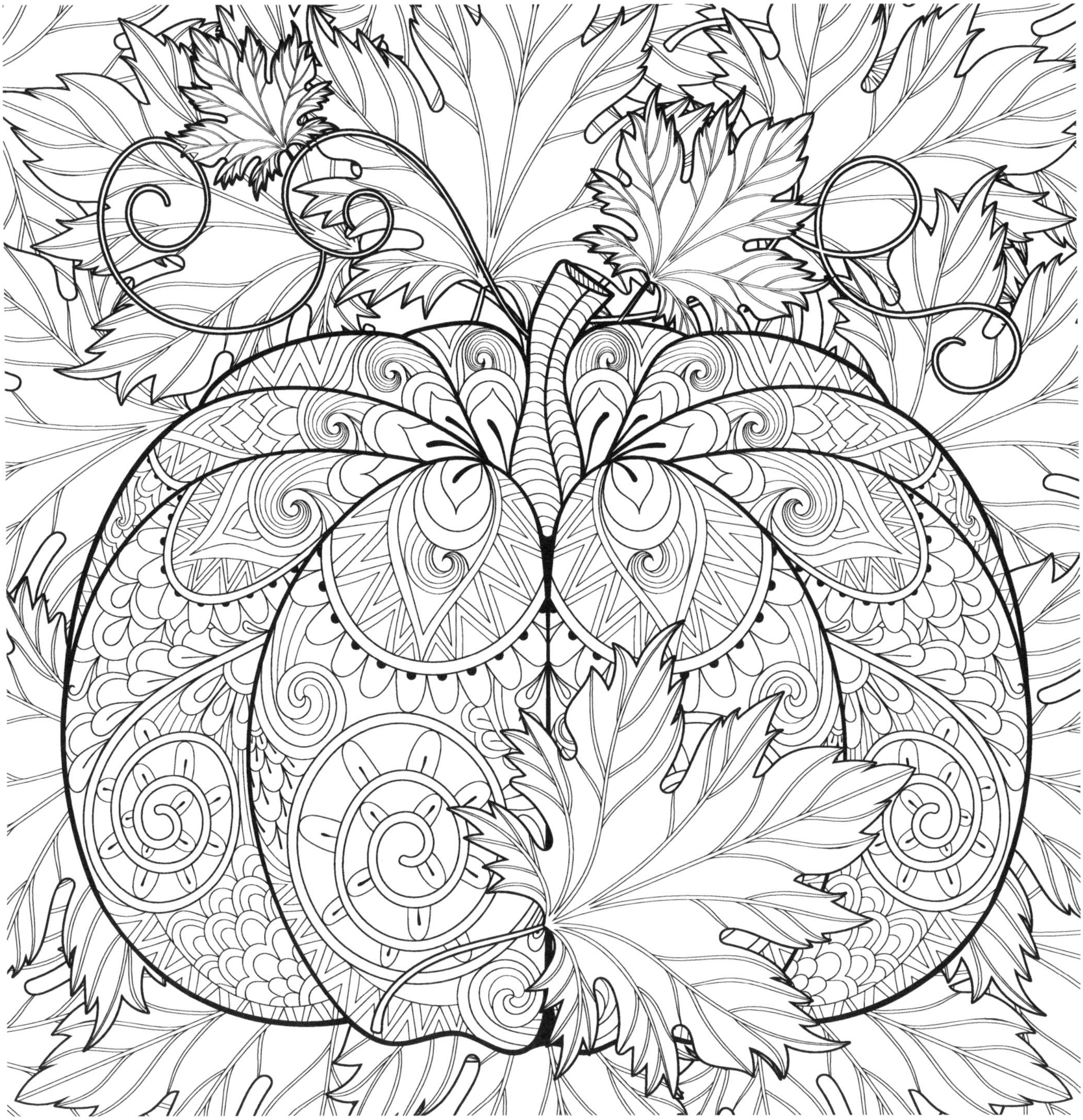

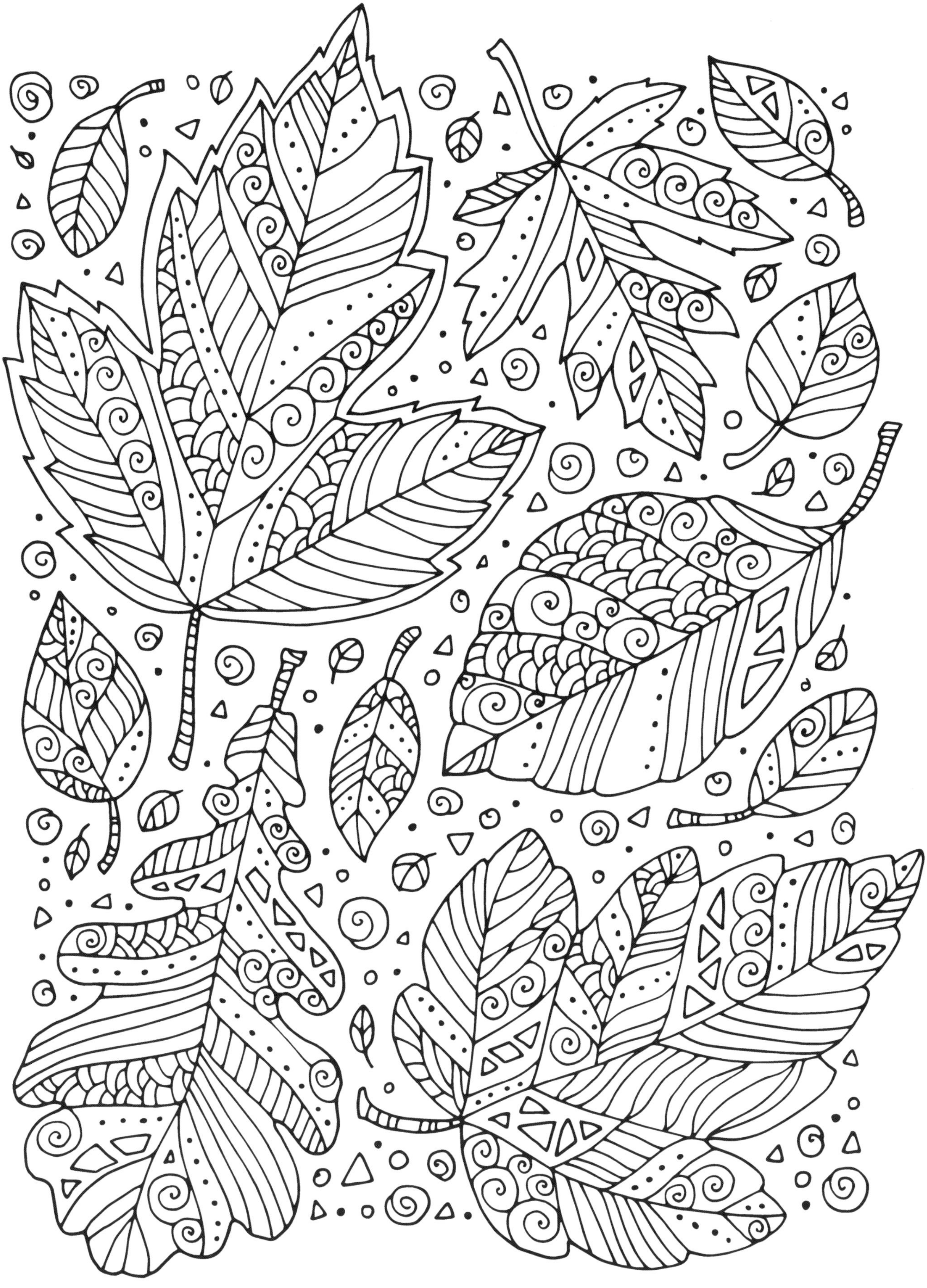

HAPPY

TURKEY

DAY

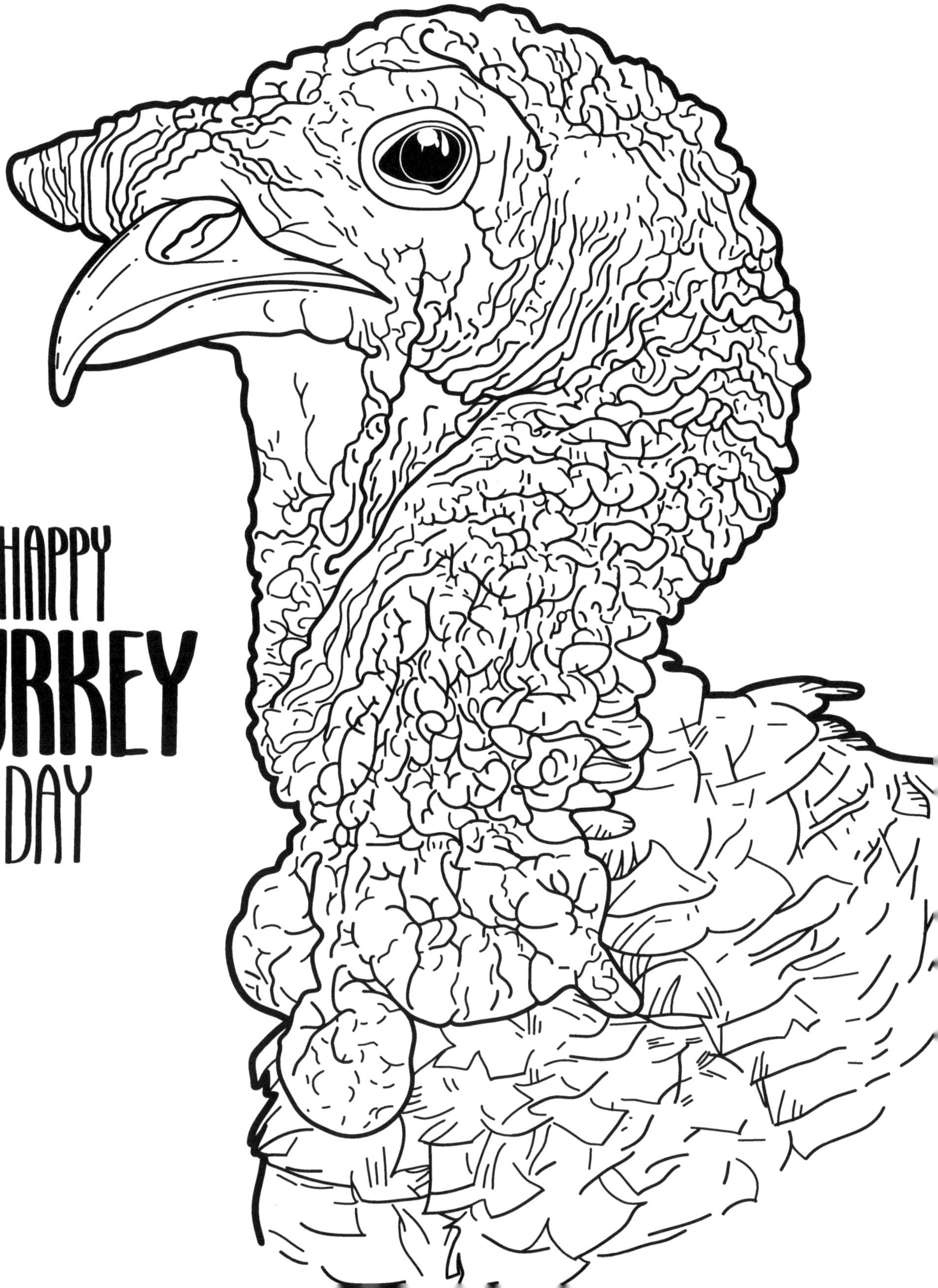

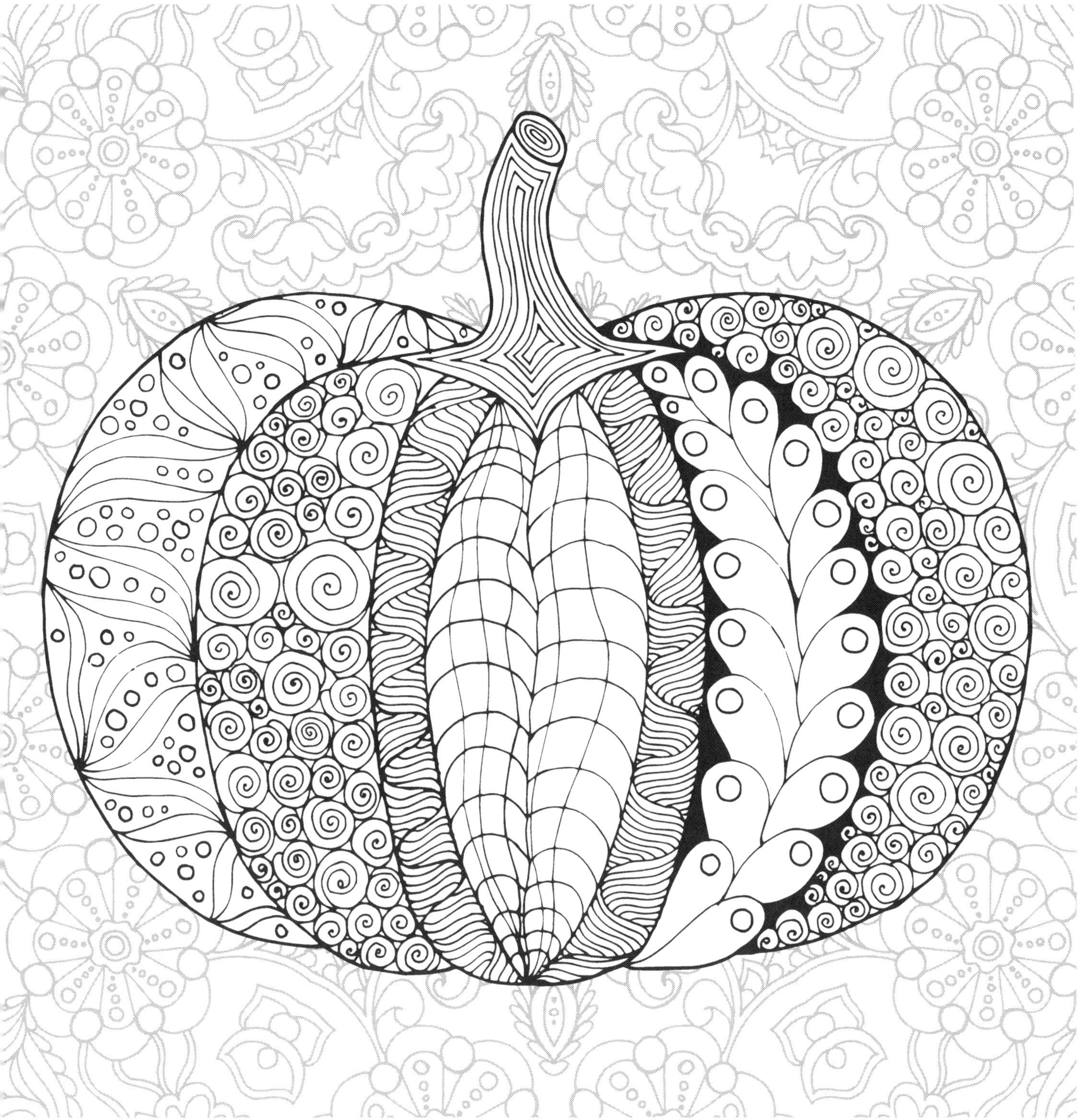

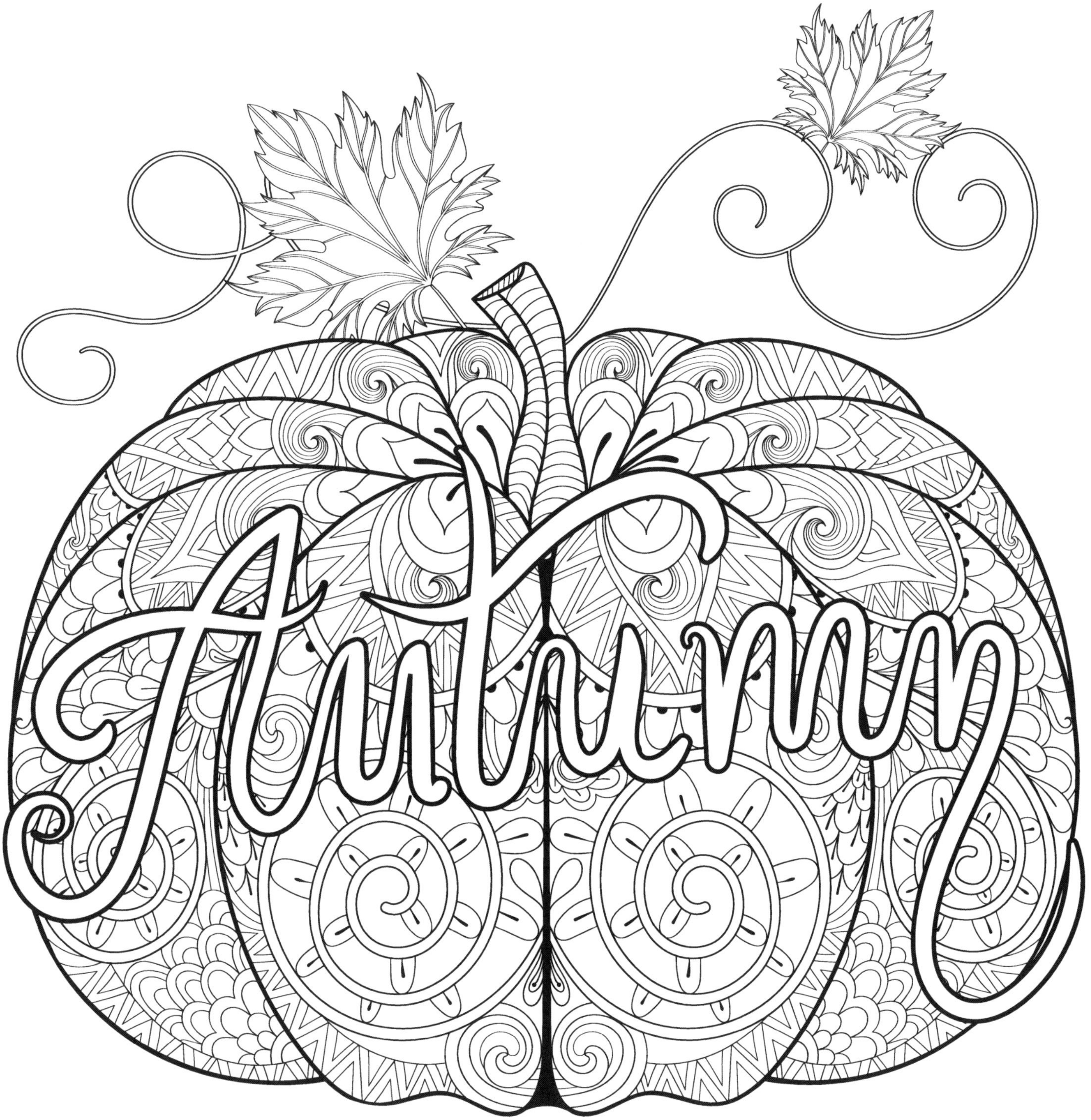
Autumn

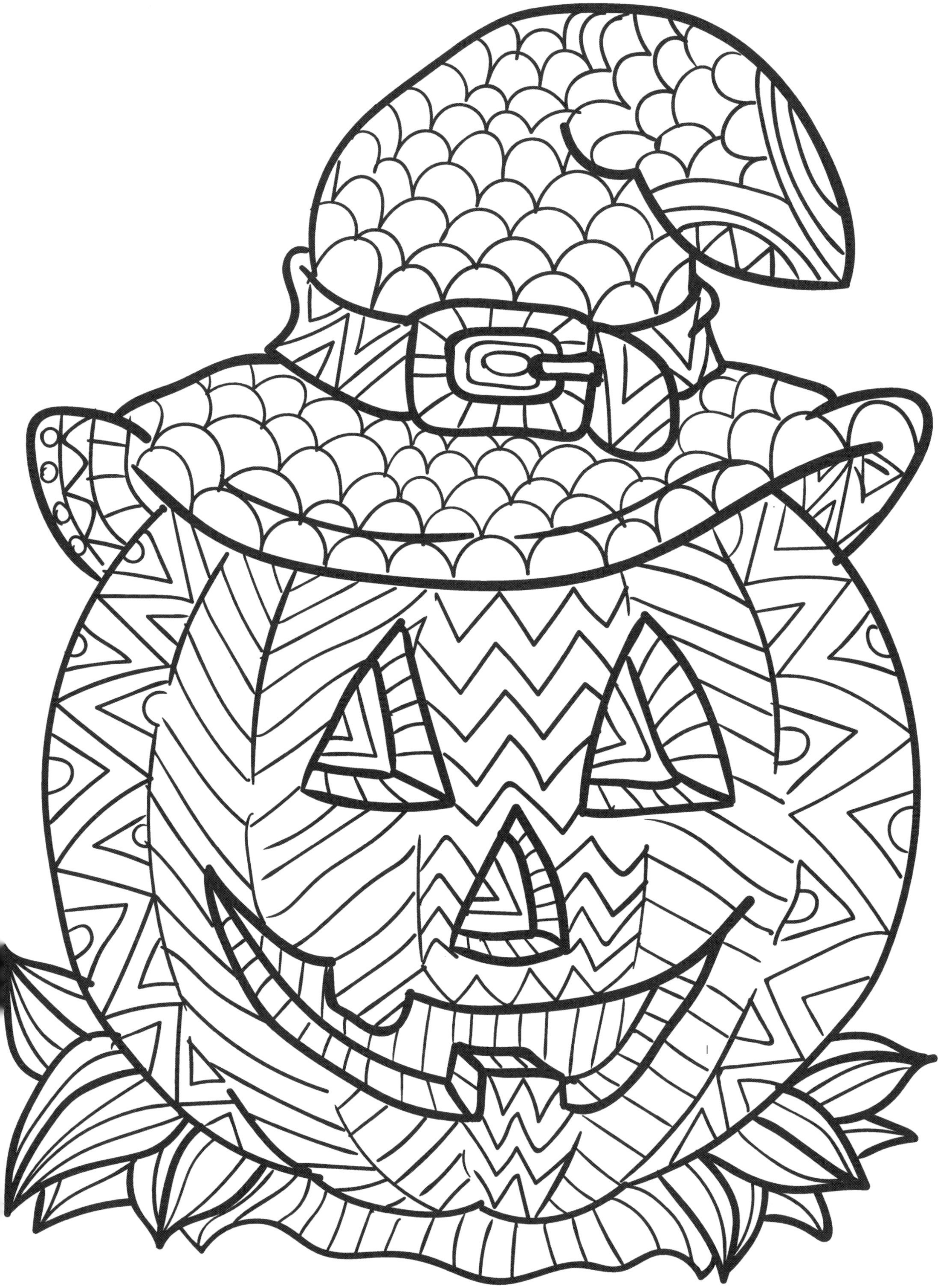

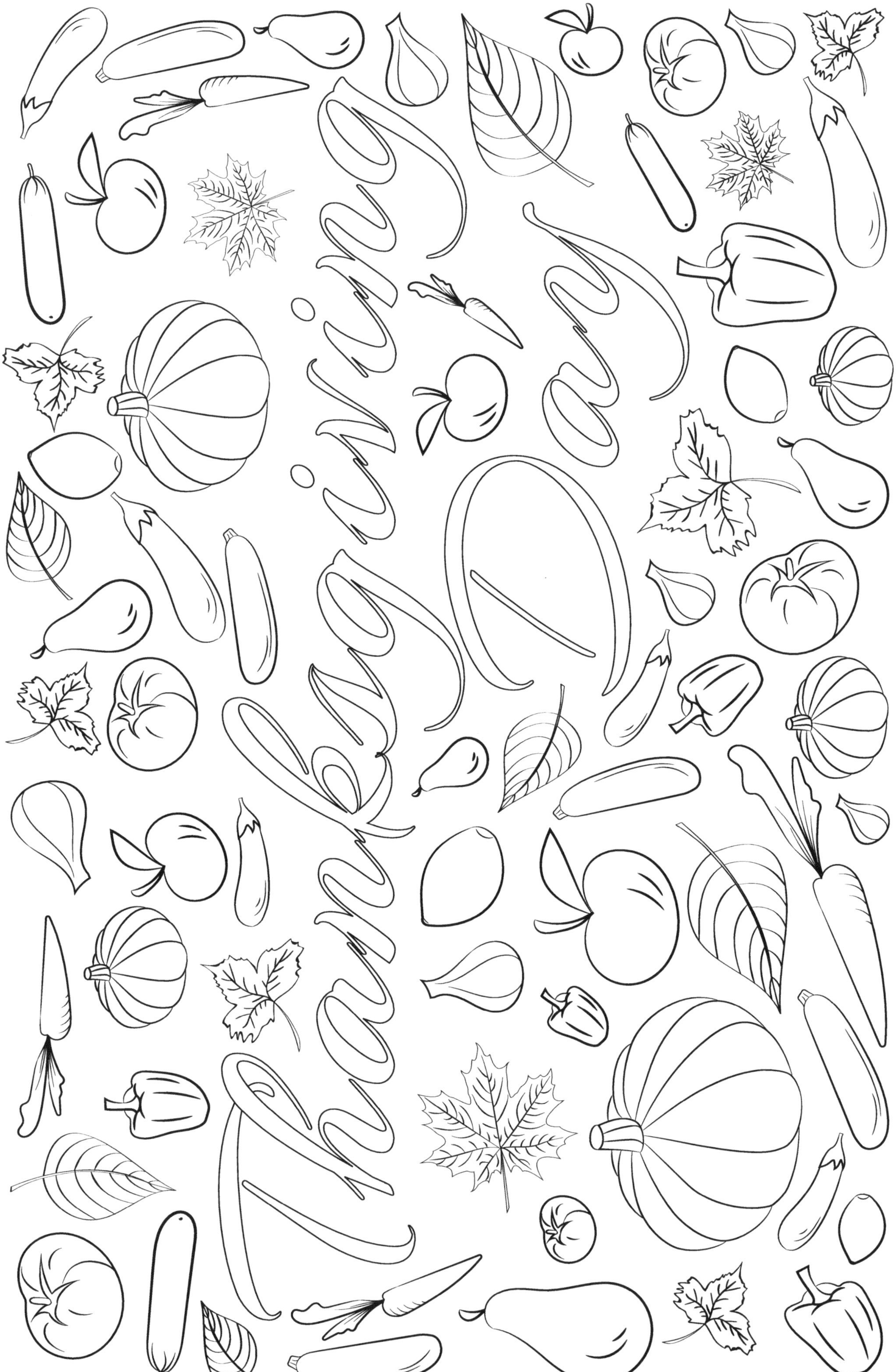
Thanksgiving Day

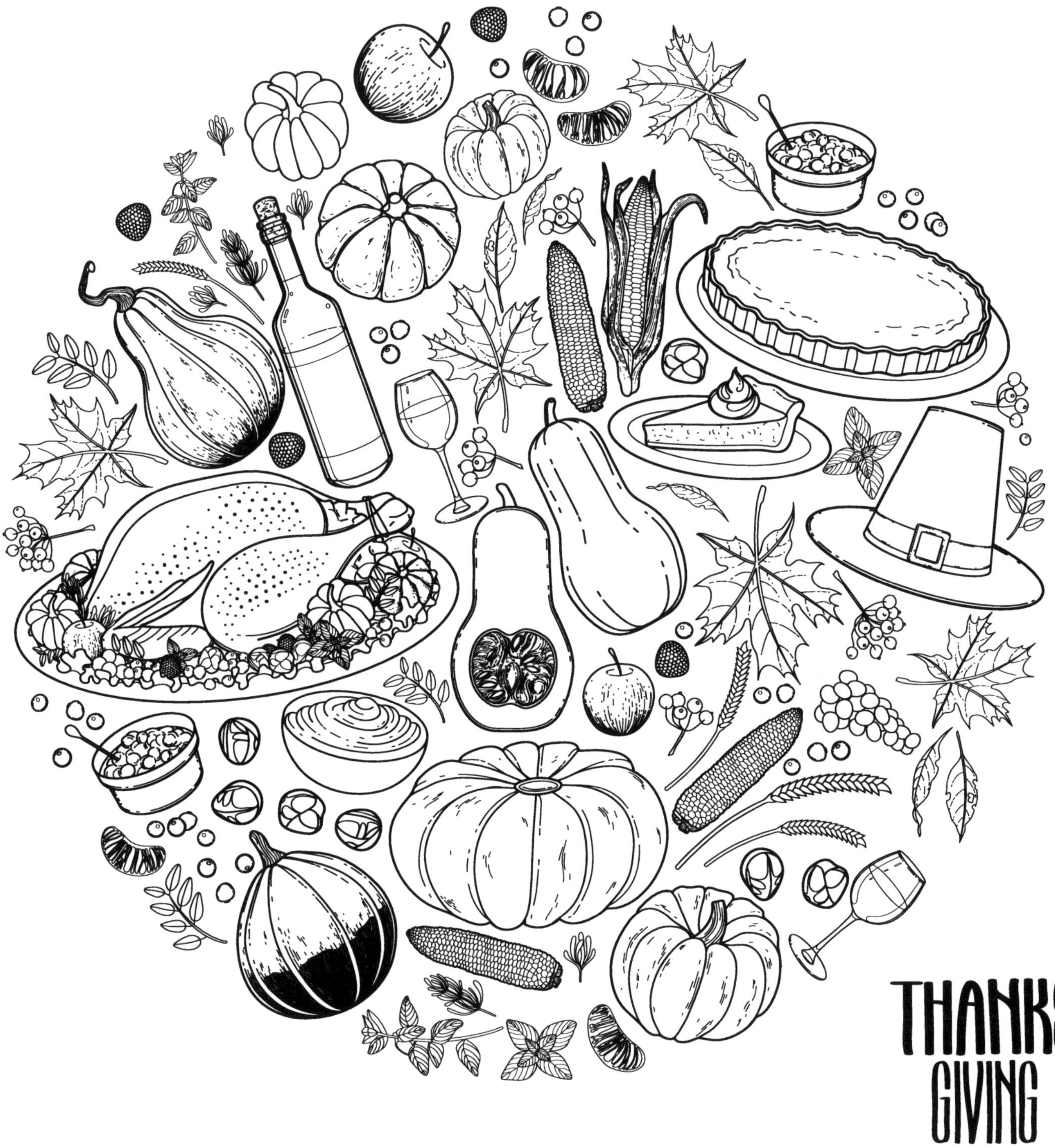

THANKS
GIVING

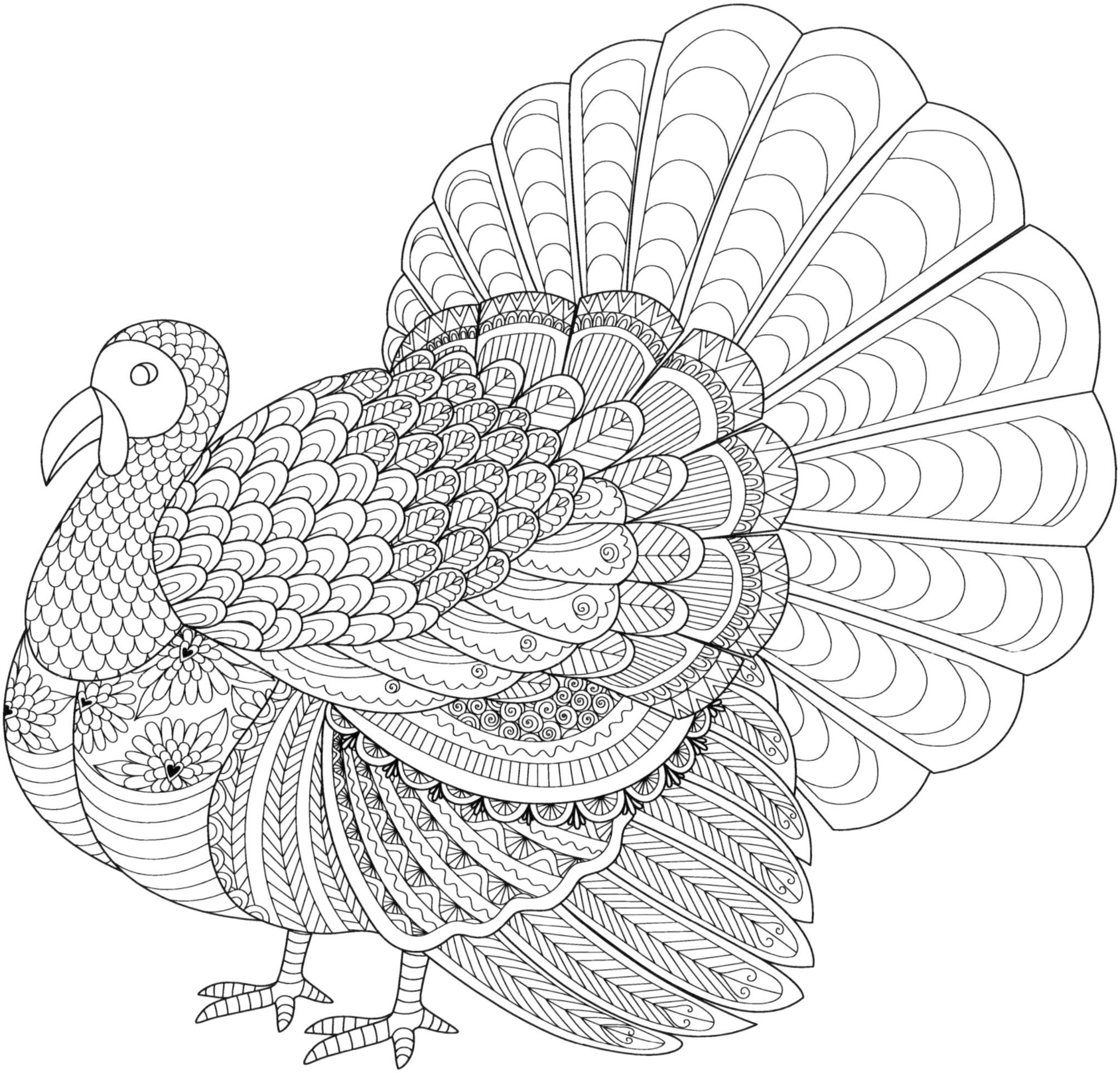

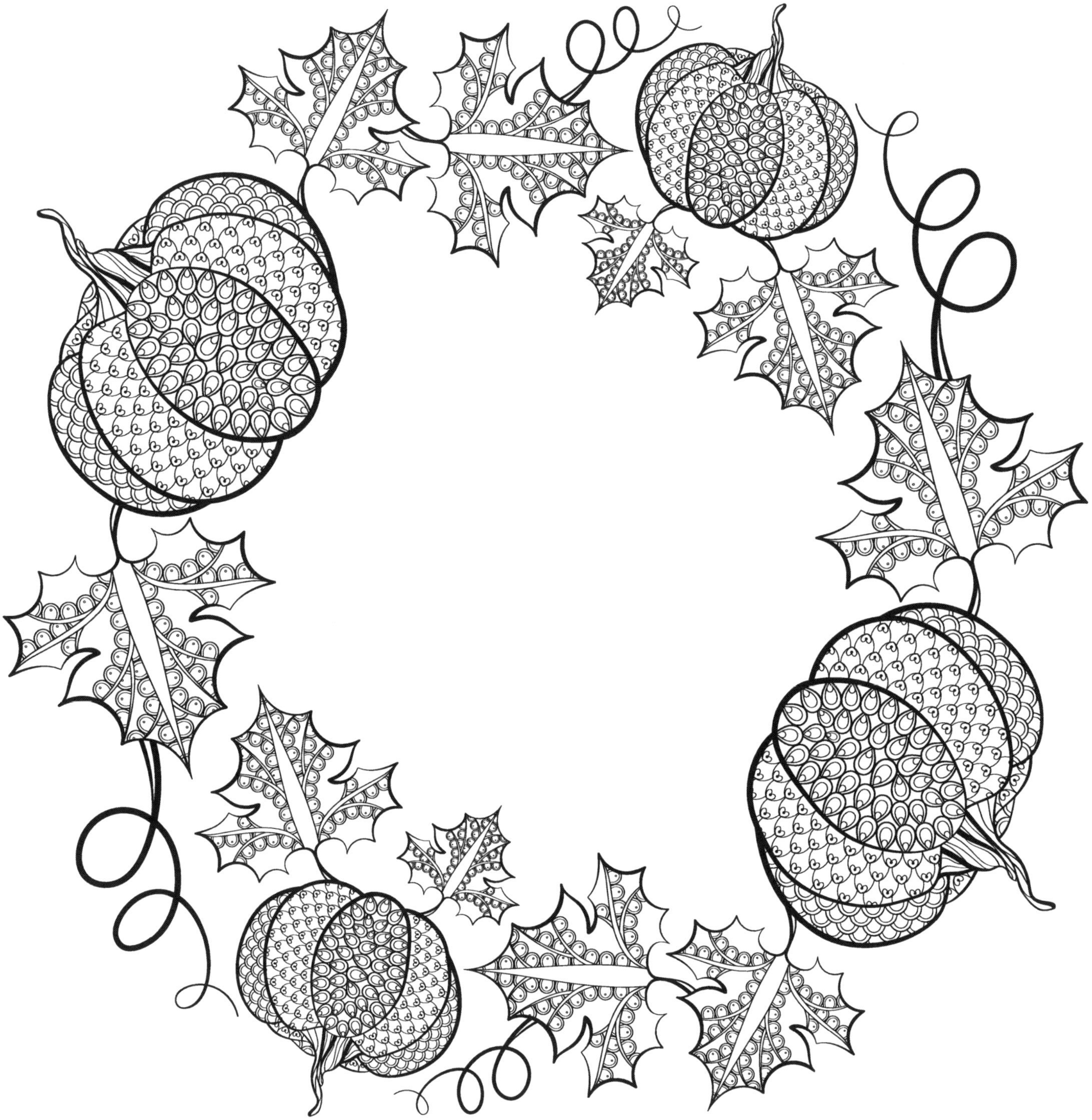

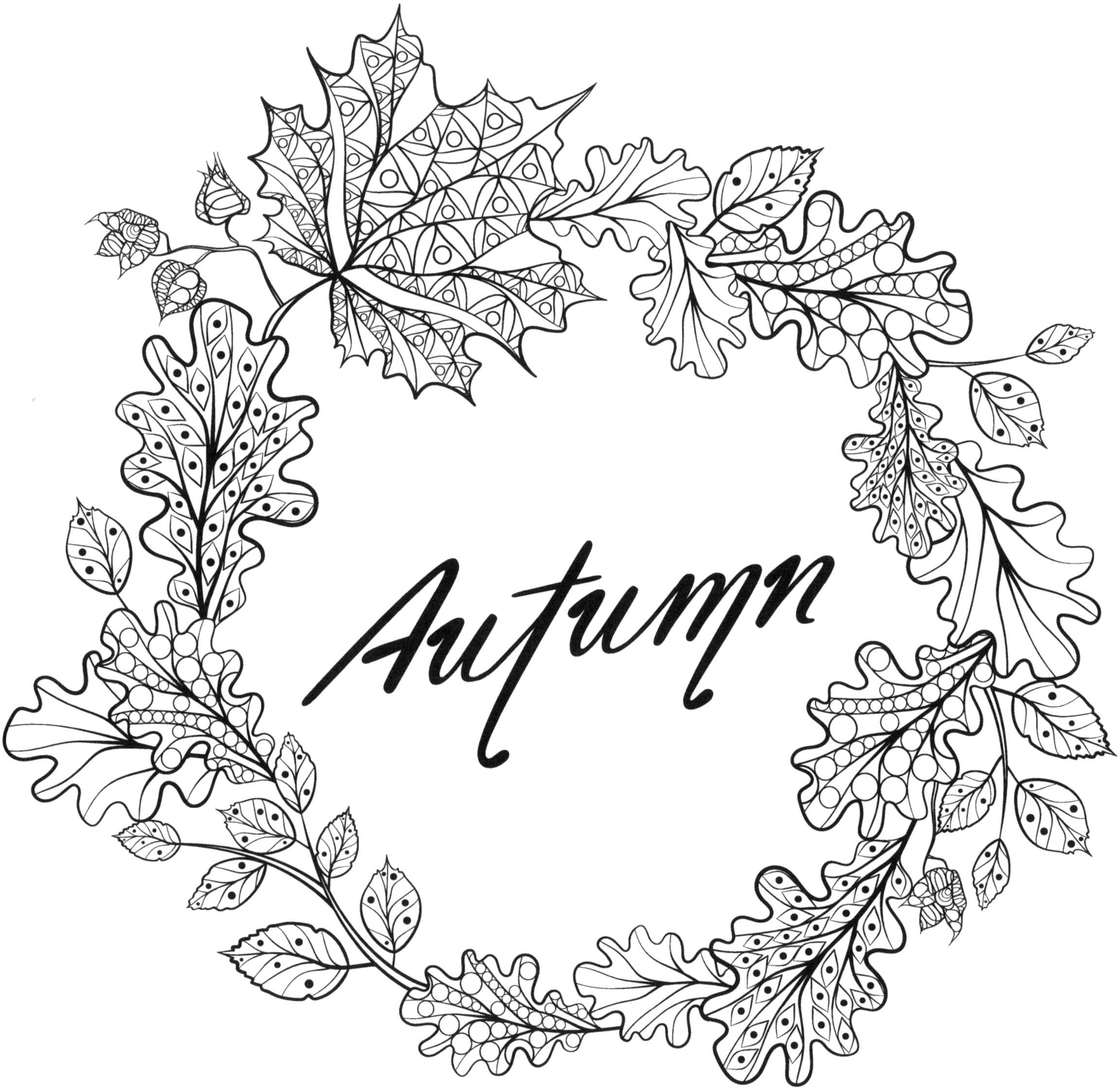
Autumn

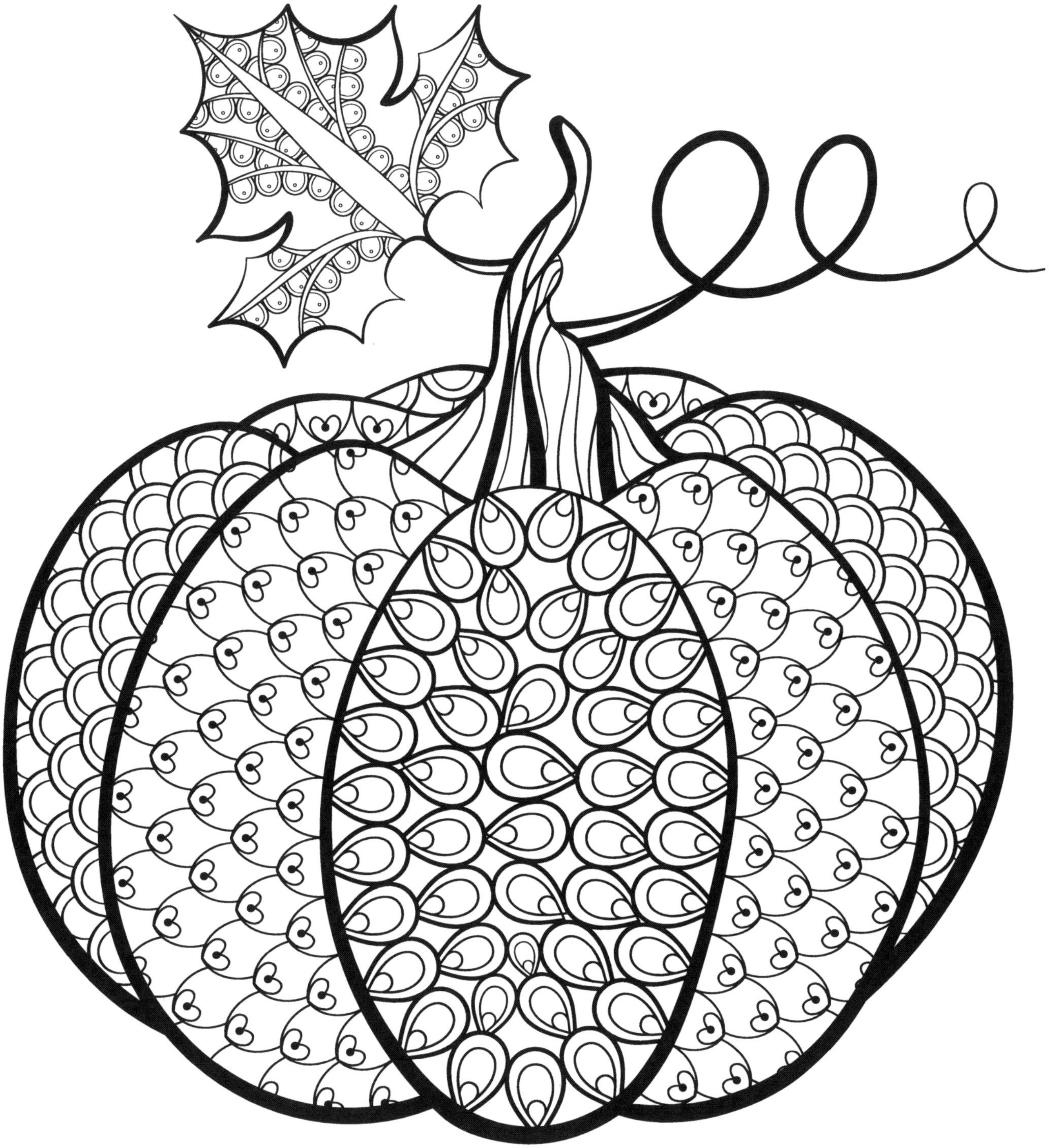

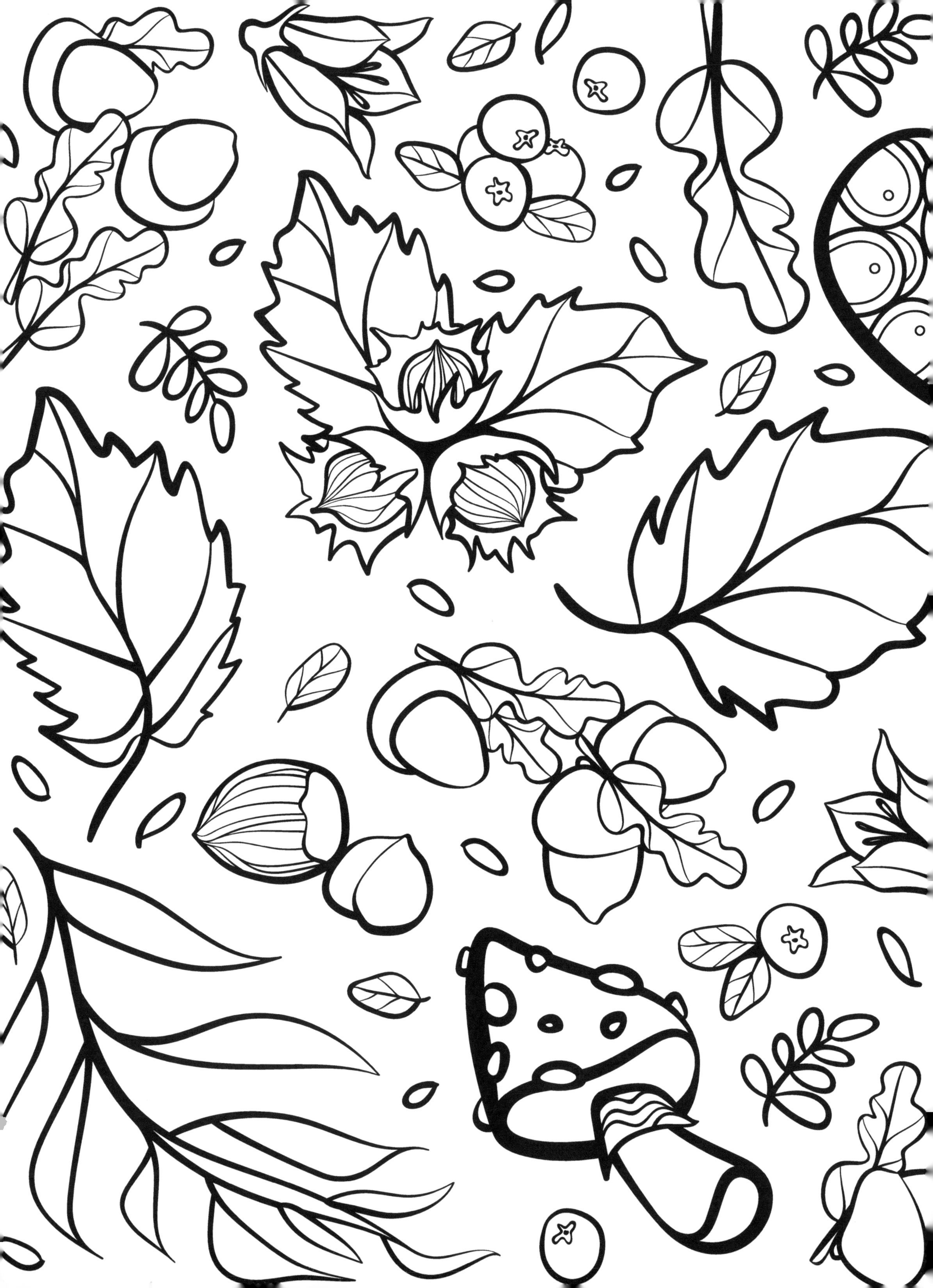

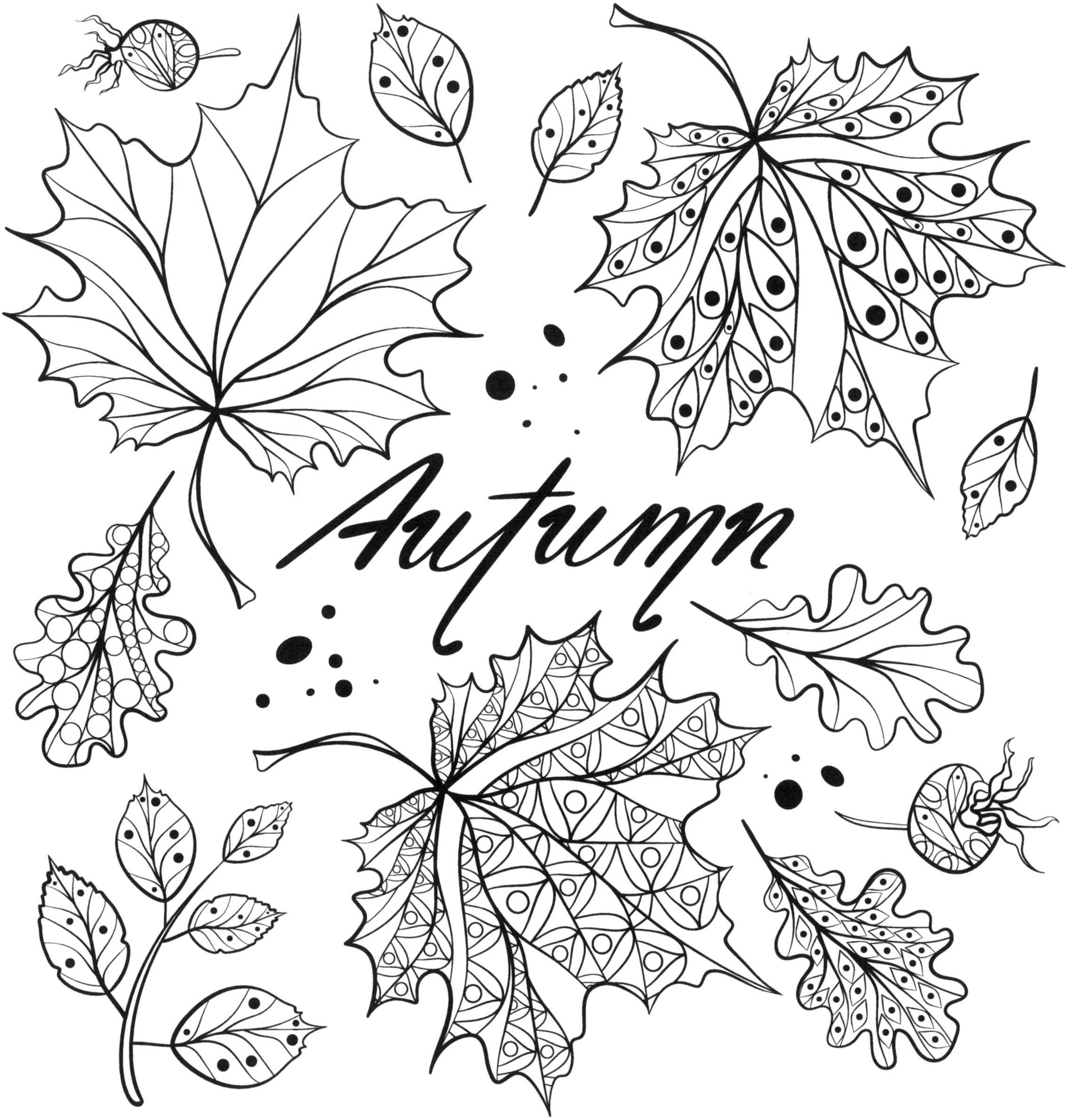
Autumn

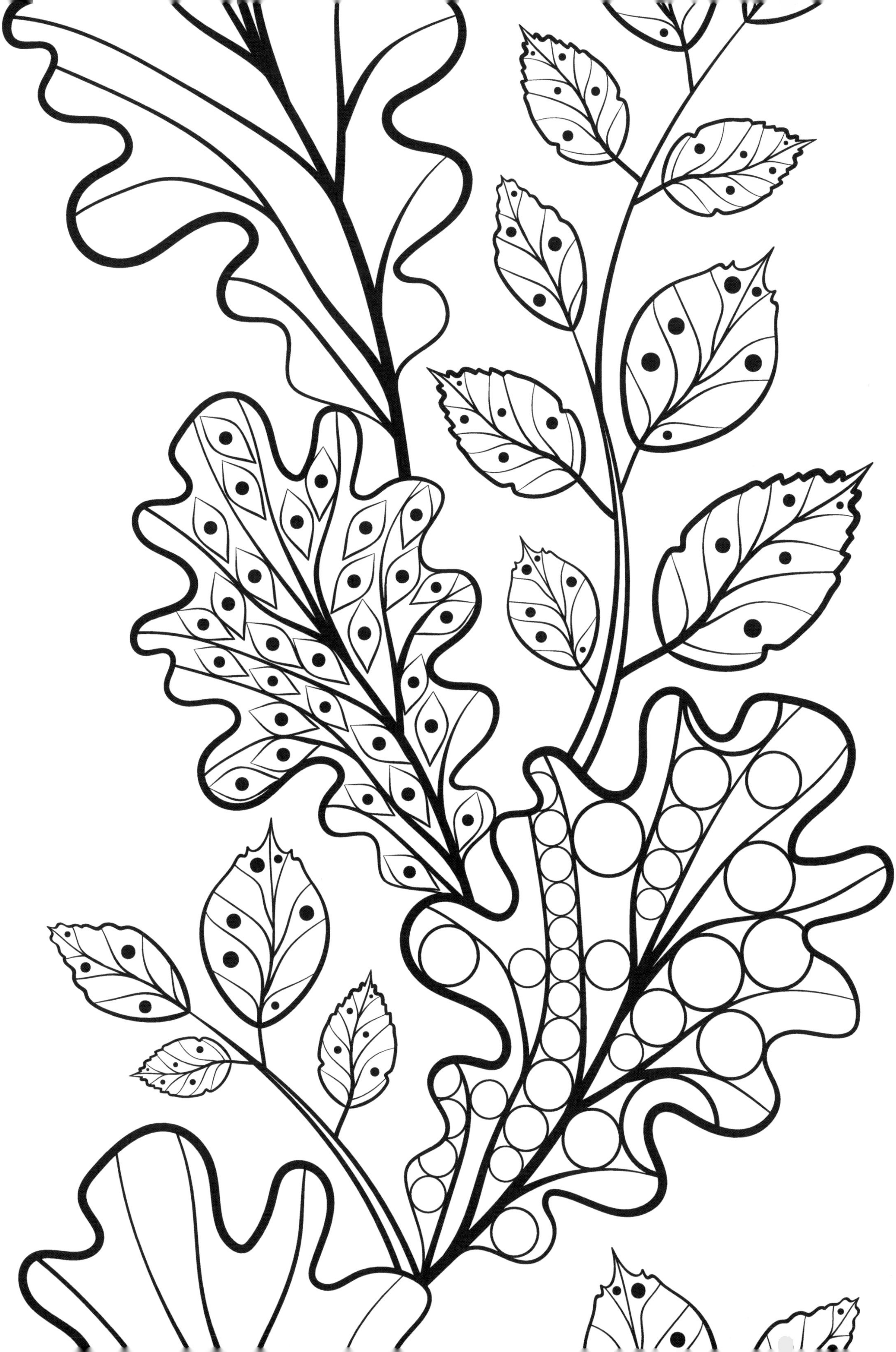

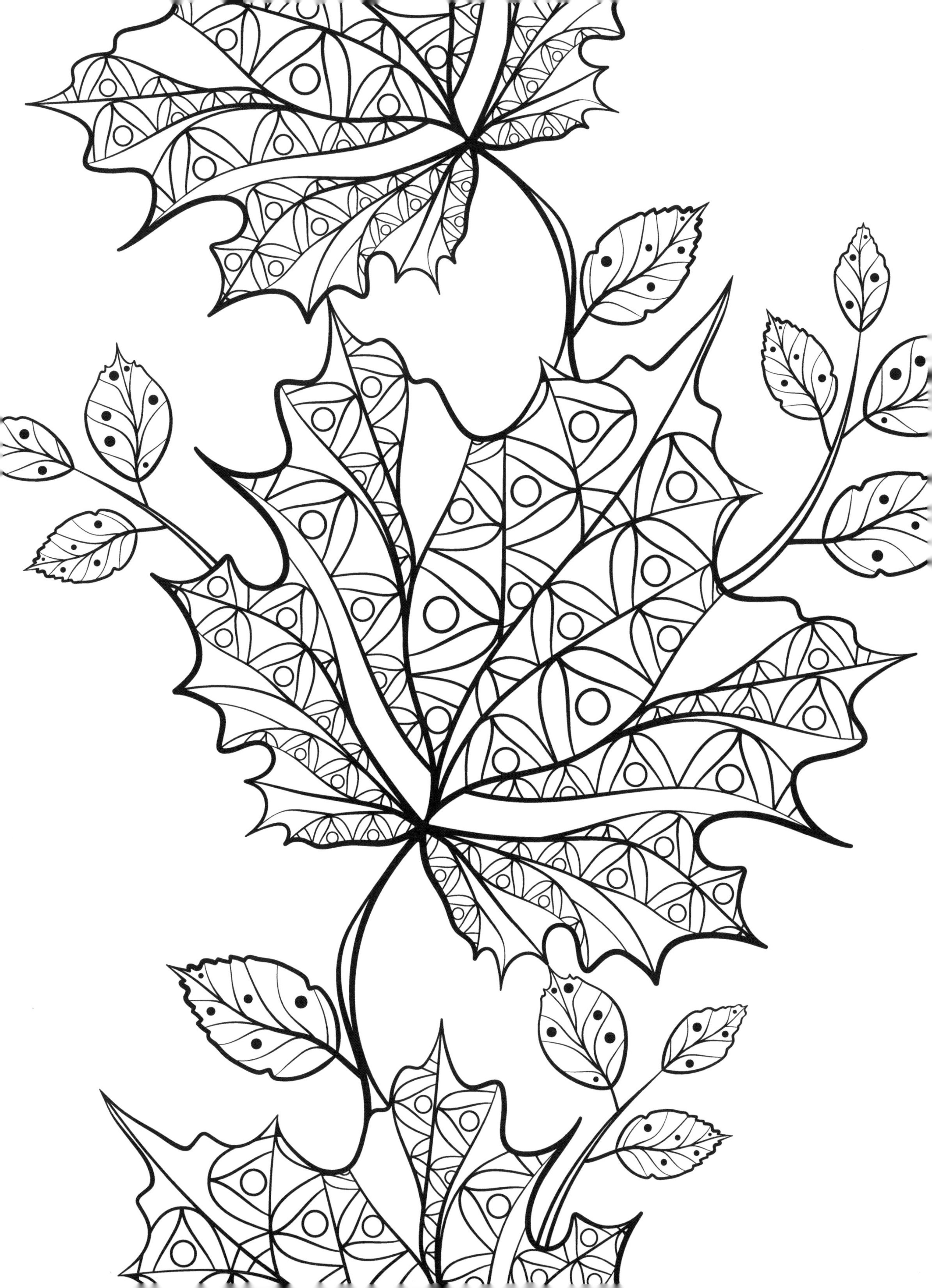

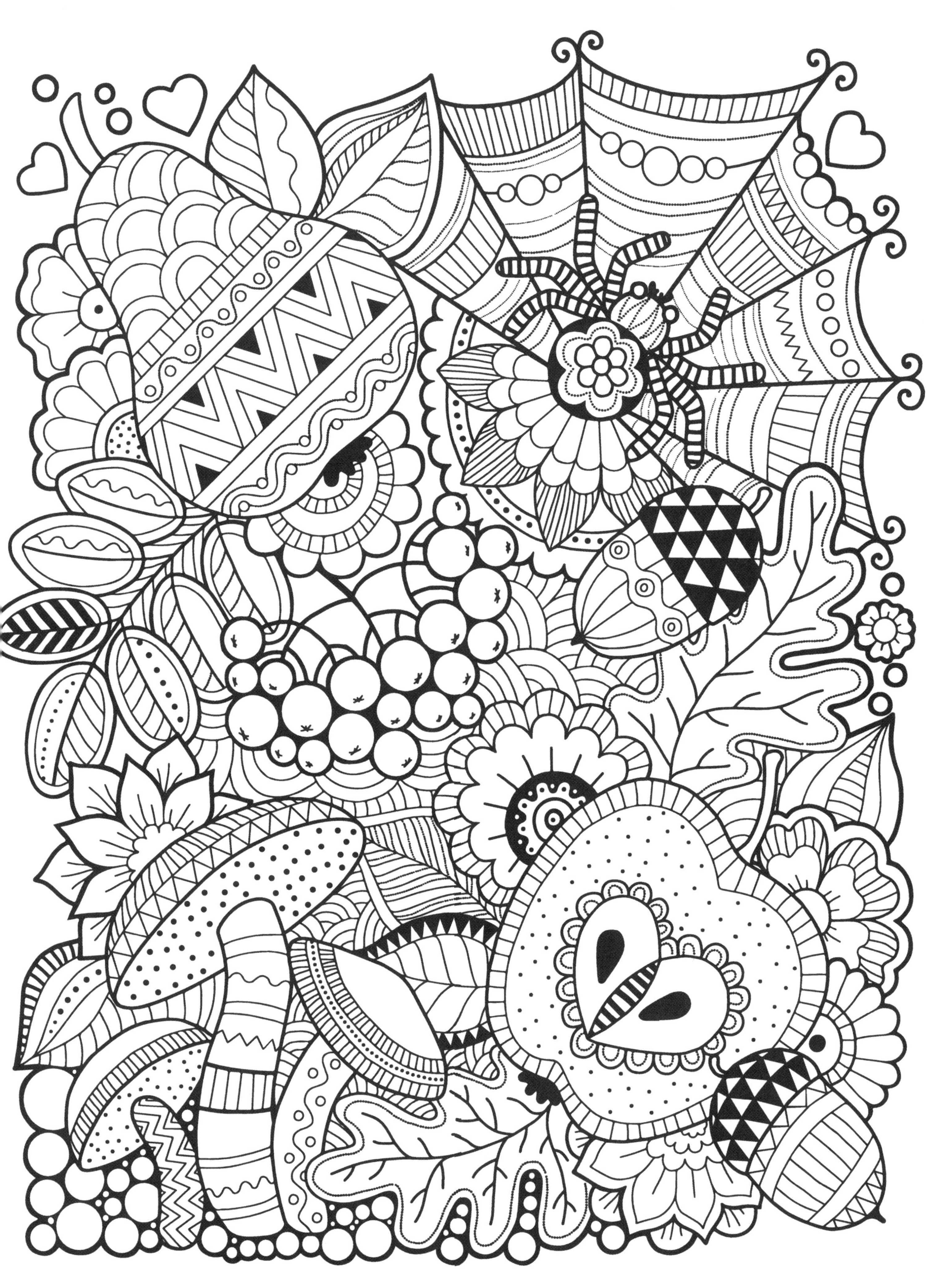

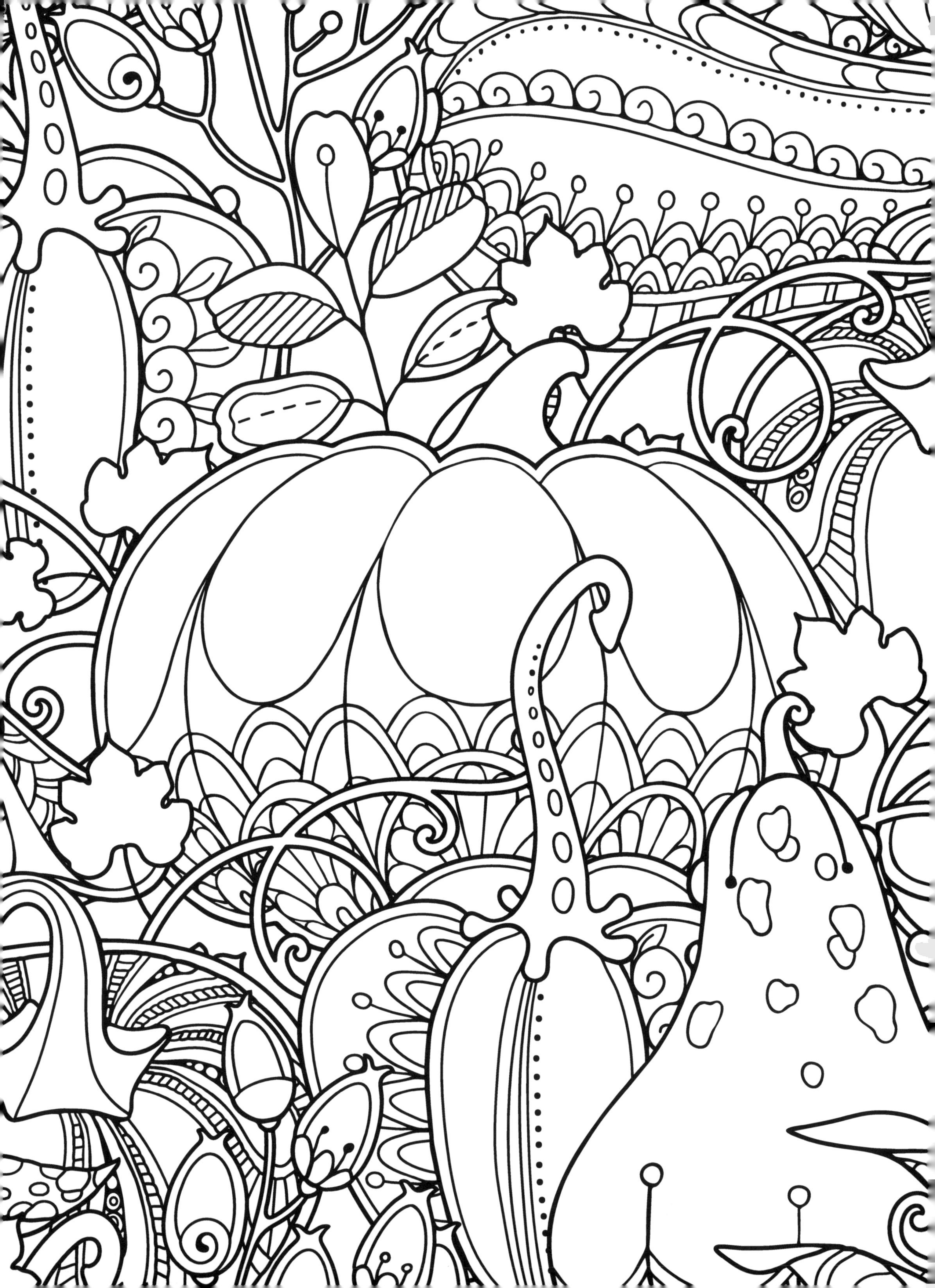

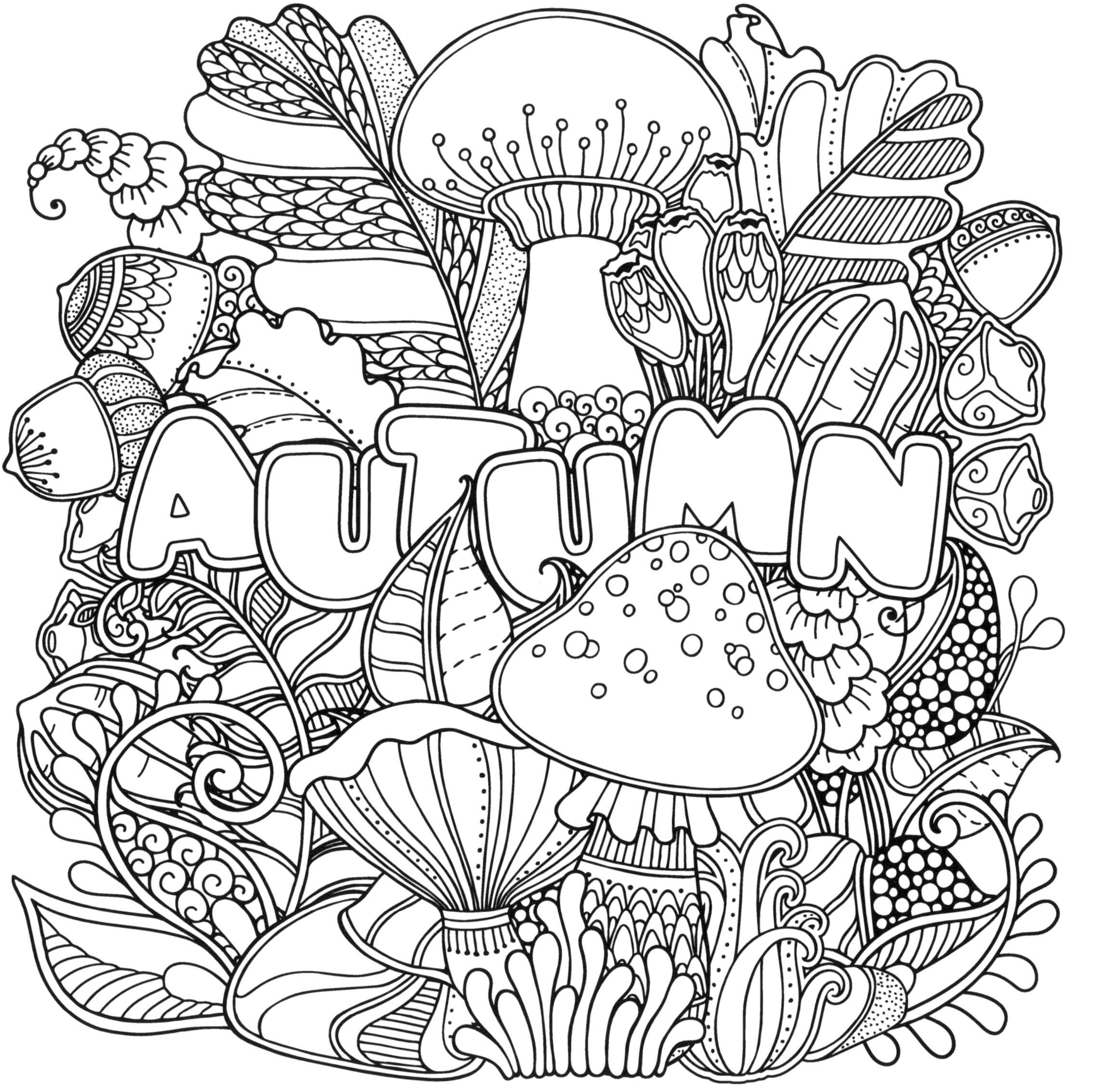
AUTUMN

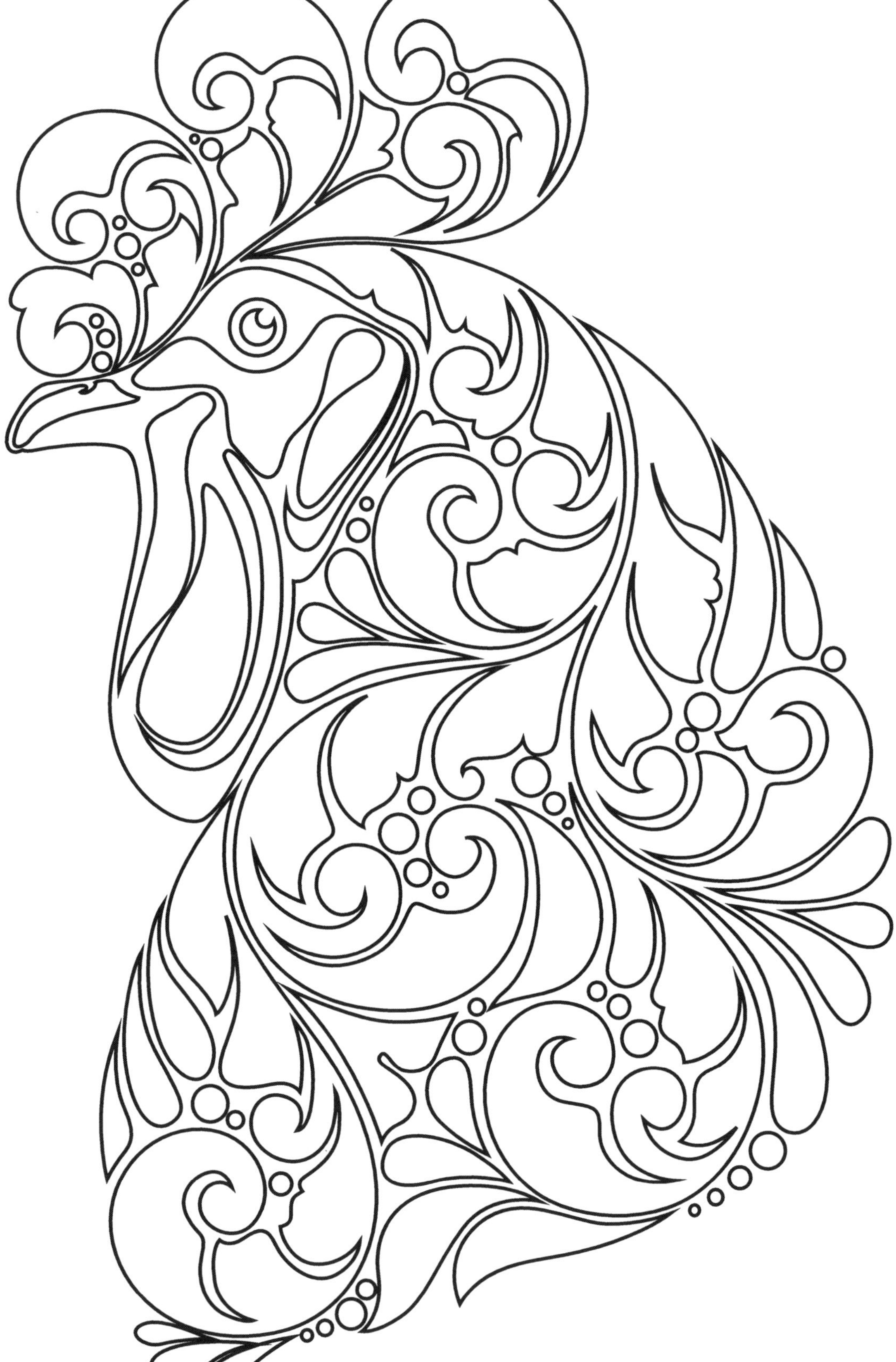

Made in the USA
Las Vegas, NV
02 January 2023

64722618R00037